AN INTRODUCTION TO
COUNTERTRANSFERENCE

AN INTRODUCTION TO
COUNTERTRANSFERENCE

CLAIRE CARTWRIGHT

Los Angeles | London | New Delhi
Singapore | Washington DC | Melbourne

Los Angeles | London | New Delhi
Singapore | Washington DC | Melbourne

SAGE Publications Ltd
1 Oliver's Yard
55 City Road
London EC1Y 1SP

SAGE Publications Inc.
2455 Teller Road
Thousand Oaks, California 91320

SAGE Publications India Pvt Ltd
B 1/I 1 Mohan Cooperative Industrial Area
Mathura Road
New Delhi 110 044

SAGE Publications Asia-Pacific Pte Ltd
3 Church Street
#10-04 Samsung Hub
Singapore 049483

Editor: Susannah Trefgarne
Assistant editor: Ruth Lilly
Production editor: Prachi Arora
Copyeditor: Christine Bitten
Indexer: KnowledgeWorks Global Ltd
Marketing manager: Dilhara Attygalle
Cover design: Naomi Robinson
Typeset by: C&M Digitals (P) Ltd, Chennai, India
Printed in the UK

Library of Congress Control Number: 2021945525

British Library Cataloguing in Publication data

A catalogue record for this book is available from
the British Library

ISBN 978-1-5264-9952-3
ISBN 978-1-5264-9951-6 (pbk)
eISBN 978-1-5297-8912-6

At SAGE we take sustainability seriously. Most of our products are printed in the UK using responsibly sourced
papers and boards. When we print overseas we ensure sustainable papers are used as measured by the PREPS
grading system. We undertake an annual audit to monitor our sustainability.

Table of Contents

About the Author

Claire Cartwright is a clinical psychologist, an Associate Professor of Clinical Psychology at the University of Auckland, and a Fellow of the New Zealand College of Clinical Psychologists. Dr Cartwright initially trained in cognitive-behavioural and psychodynamic therapy approaches. Early on in her teaching of trainee therapists, Dr Cartwright observed that trainees often experience difficulty recognising, understanding, and managing countertransference reactions. She began experimenting with ways to make countertransference theory and practice accessible to trainees and therapists from a range of therapeutic approaches. This began the development of the approach to countertransference that she introduces in this book. For the last fifteen years, Dr Cartwright's primary teaching and research focus has been on countertransference. Along with colleagues, she has conducted and published research into teaching and learning about countertransference. She has presented her research at several international conferences and offered training workshops for mental health professionals in understanding and managing countertransference therapeutically.

Preface

This book introduces countertransference and is designed to be accessible to therapists and trainees from different psychotherapeutic approaches who would like to enhance their knowledge and practice in relation to countertransference. Research conducted in the last two decades supports the view, long held by psychoanalytic/psychodynamic therapists, that countertransference reactions can have negative effects on the therapeutic relationship and therapy outcomes, while understanding and managing countertransference can benefit the therapeutic relationship and therapy outcomes.

The notion of countertransference was first introduced by Freud and developed mainly within psychoanalytic/psychodynamic paradigms. However, therapists from all schools of psychotherapy experience countertransference although they may use other terms to describe these reactions. There is a rich psychoanalytic and psychodynamic literature on countertransference. This literature, however, is often complex and difficult to understand for those who are new to the world of countertransference. The literature may also be experienced as inaccessible to therapists and trainees from other schools of psychotherapy. This book aims to address these issues.

Over the last 15 years, I have developed and researched an approach to conceptualising and managing countertransference that I have taught to trainees and therapists in classroom situations, workshops, and in individual and group supervision. The approach integrates research and clinical literature relevant to understanding and managing countertransference with my own clinical and teaching experience. It is influenced mainly by psychodynamic conceptions of countertransference but uses accessible language and concepts that are easily understood from other perspectives. It places emphasis on managing the potentially problematic aspects of countertransference and enhancing the positive aspects. As part of this, the book introduces a systematic approach to using countertransference as a tool for understanding the client's experiences in therapy.

Chapter 1 provides an historical overview of the conceptualisation of countertransference, beginning with Freud's classical view through to more recent perspectives. The status of countertransference in cognitive-behavioural therapy and integrative psychotherapies is also discussed. Chapter 2 considers the role of countertransference within the therapeutic relationship, examines the range of countertransference reactions reported by therapists and trainees, and defines different types of countertransference (negative and positive;

subjective and objective). The chapter then introduces cultural transference and countertransference and ends with a discussion of ethical and professional issues using therapeutic vignettes.

Chapters 3 and 4 present a four-step approach to understanding and managing countertransference, and illustrate the approach with case studies and therapy vignettes. These steps include monitoring and being aware of countertransference responses, reflecting on clients' patterns of relating to others, developing hypotheses about the interpersonal processes (transference and countertransference), and managing countertransference reactions as they arise in sessions. The Parent–Adult–Child (PAC) model that originated in Transactional Analysis is used to provide a visual representation of transference and countertransference reactions. Chapter 4 also considers two case studies of countertransference from a CBT perspective to illustrate the four-step approach applied to a different therapeutic model.

Chapter 5 addresses processes that lead to the development and repair of disruptions or ruptures to the therapeutic alliance. Transference and countertransference issues often contribute to or underlie therapeutic disruptions. The chapter examines therapeutic events that can lead to disruptions, signs that the client is experiencing a disruption to the alliance with the therapist, and a series of activities that the therapist can engage in to resolve or repair the disruption or rupture. Once again, therapeutic vignettes are used to illustrate these processes and therapeutic interventions.

Chapter 6 discusses in greater depth the activities that therapists can engage in to manage countertransference therapeutically. This includes discussion of reflective practice activities, breathing and mindfulness meditation, the use of formulation to assist in conceptualising interactions with clients, the use of empathic self-talk, and a process of moving back into the Adult (PAC model). This chapter also discusses managing sexual countertransference using the four-step approach. The chapter ends with a discussion of the issues around sharing countertransference reactions with clients.

Chapter 7 discusses and illustrates the application of the four-step approach in classroom, group supervision, or workshop situations. The chapter also provides a revision of the strategies used throughout the book to understand and manage countertransference. It will be of assistance to supervisors and teachers who would like to teach the approach in classrooms or in workshops, and to groups of colleagues who want to work together on understanding and managing countertransference.

Acknowledgements

I would like to thank those people who have supported me to write this book. Thank you to the people at Sage Publishers, especially my editor Susannah Trefgarne who immediately liked the idea of an introduction to countertransference, was enthusiastic about the original proposal for this book, and remained so throughout its development. Thank you also to Ruth Lilly for her editorial assistance throughout this process. I enjoyed and valued our contact. And thank you to my husband Richard who has always been supportive and encouraging about my work, and to my daughter Jess for her love and support.

Over the last 10 years I have had a number of collaborators in Australia and New Zealand who have engaged in research projects with me in relation to my approach to teaching countertransference. Thank you to the colleagues and trainees from Waikato University, University of Canterbury, Massey University, Victoria University, University of Otago, Sydney University of Technology, University of New South Wales, and Queensland University of Technology who have supported this countertransference research. Thank you also to Jeff Hayes from Penn State University for engaging me in the study of your five-component model of countertransference and to the Australian and New Zealand colleagues who also contributed to this.

I would especially like to acknowledge my colleagues in the clinical psychology programme in the School of Psychology at the University of Auckland who supported and valued my teaching and research in countertransference. Thank you also to the University of Auckland clinical psychology trainees who engaged with the reflective practice activities presented in this book. I really enjoyed working with you on countertransference challenges and I am impressed by the dedication you gave to understanding and managing your reactions to clients. Your questions, comments, and ideas have enriched my understanding of countertransference. I could not have written this book without you.

1

An Introduction to Countertransference

This chapter presents a brief overview of the historical development of the concept of countertransference within psychoanalytic/psychodynamic paradigms. It begins with Freud's classic view of countertransference as a potential impediment to therapy, examines the development of the totalistic view of countertransference in the late 1940s and 1950s, and then considers more modern conceptualisations. A number of related concepts are introduced, including objective and subjective countertransference, and complementary and concordant countertransference.

In line with a main aim of this book to present an introduction to countertransference that is accessible to therapists from different therapeutic schools, the final section of the chapter reflects on cognitive-behavioural therapy (CBT) and integrative perspectives of countertransference. The chapter ends with a discussion of the areas of agreement and disagreement in relation to countertransference and presents the conceptualisation of countertransference that is used in this book.

Psychodynamic perspectives of countertransference

Freud's classical view

In 1938, the year before his death, Sigmund Freud reflected back on the development of his psychoanalytic theory (Freud, 2003). Freud wrote that as an analyst, he would have been content to have a role something akin to that of an alpine guide assisting the patient on a difficult mountain climb. However, in his work as an analyst he soon found that this was not possible. For the patient, he wrote, the analyst represents an important figure from his child-hood and the patient transfers the feelings associated with this figure on to the therapist. Freud named this process transference. Freud initially viewed trans-ference as a form of resistance but in time also came to view it as an important analytic tool. Through the experience of the transference to the analyst, the patient's past was brought alive and made conscious, and through the ana-lyst's work with the transference the patient could be freed from the past. However, the transference involved strong emotional attachments and also ambivalent feelings towards the analyst, which were challenging for both.

Freud spoke or wrote about countertransference on only a few occasions. He first used the term countertransference (*Gegenübertragung*) in a letter to Carl Jung dated 7 June 1909 (McGuire, 1974) in which he appeared to normalise or reassure Jung about intense emotional reactions and attachments that can happen in psychoanalysis. In reply to Jung, Freud wrote that these intense emotional experiences 'help us to develop the thick skin we need to dominate "counter-transference", which is after all a permanent problem for us' (p. 145). These words of Freud revealed that Freud himself experienced countertrans-ference reactions, saw these reactions as an ongoing challenge, and believed that the analyst should work to 'dominate' these reactions.

Freud first mentioned countertransference publicly at the Second Psychoanalytic Congress held at Nuremberg in 1910 in which he was addressing innovations in psychoanalytic technique. He said: 'We have become aware of the "counter-transference", which arises in [the analyst] as a result of the patient's influence on his unconscious feelings, and we are almost inclined to insist that he shall recognise this counter-transference in himself and overcome it' (Freud, Strachey, & Freud, 1973, pp. 144–145). Freud then suggested to his audience that it was essential that they undertake their own self-analyses.

In 1915, in writing about 'transference-love', Freud warned other analysts about any counter-transference reactions they might have to patients falling in love with them, and to remember that the patient's 'falling in love is induced

The classical view

Freud's view of countertransference is now known as the classical view. According to this classical view, countertransference feelings arise in the ana-lyst as a result of the patient's influence on the analyst's unconscious. These unconscious reactions of the analyst need to be overcome or dominated for the sake of the patient and the analysis. In order to be able to achieve this, analysts were advised to undertake an intensive process of self-analysis.

by the analytic situation' and 'not the charms of his own person' (Freud, 1993, p. 174). Freud also expressed concern in the same paper that the lay public would be concerned about discussions of countertransference. This may be one of the reasons why Freud so rarely talked about countertransference.

However, there is also some evidence that Freud saw potential for positive aspects in the analyst's emotional responses to the client. Freud spoke of counter-transference again in a letter to Ludwig Binswanger dated 20 February 1913:

> The problem of counter-transference ... is – technically – among the most intricate in psychoanalysis. Theoretically I believe it is much easier to solve. What we give to the patient should, however, be a spontaneous affect, but measured out consciously at all times, to a greater or lesser extent according to need. In certain circum-stances a great deal, but never one's own unconscious. I would look upon that as the formula. One must, therefore, always recognise one's counter-transference and overcome it, for not till then is one free oneself. (letter 86f, 20 February 1913, in Fichtner, 2003, p. 112)

This letter gives a glimpse into Freud's more nuanced view of countertransfer-ence reactions to clients. Freud talks about giving 'spontaneous affect' to patients and in some instances, this might be 'a great deal'. But he emphasised the importance of not acting out on unconscious reactions and recognises that in practice, this is one of 'the most intricate' activities in psychoanalysis.

Freud's emphasis on dominating or overcoming countertransference may have reflected his concerns about the intensity of relationships developing between male psychoanalysts and their mainly female patients. However, it appears to have led to countertransference as being seen as an impediment to therapy, and negativity and anxiety within psychoanalysis in relation to the analyst's personal subjective responses. As a result of this, this classical view of countertransference was maintained for some decades and the phenomena of countertransference did not attract significant interest or focus until the late 1940s when the view of countertransference as an impediment to therapy was challenged by a number of psychoanalysts. During the 1940s and 1950s, the totalistic view of counter-transference emerged.

The totalistic perspective

In the late 1940s and 1950s a number of psychoanalysts began exploring the concept of countertransference afresh. Winnicott (1949), Heimann (1950), and Racker (1957), among others, contributed to the development of a new and influential view of countertransference (Epstein & Feiner, 1988). In 1949, Paula Heimann, who was influenced by the development of object relations theory, presented a paper titled 'On counter-transference' at the 16th Inter-national Psychoanalytic Congress in Zurich. The paper was also published the following year (Heimann, 1950). Heimann critiqued the notion of the 'good' therapist who was 'detached' in her attitude and therapeutic work. Heimann

(1950) used the term 'counter-transference' to 'cover all of the feelings which the analyst experiences towards his patient' (p. 81), thereby leading to use of the term totalistic perspective. She also argued that the therapist's total emotional response to the client is 'one of the (therapist's) most important tools' as these responses are a 'mirror reflection' of the patient's experiences in therapy and provide information and insight into the client's unconscious reactions (p. 81).

According to Heimann, the therapist's unconscious understands and responds to the client in a way that the conscious mind cannot. Countertransference reactions alert the therapist to aspects of the client's experience before the therapist is consciously aware of this. Heimann also argued that Freud's assertion that the therapist must 'recognise and master' the countertransference did not suggest that the therapist become unfeeling. According to Heimann, the role of the therapist's own analysis was to facilitate the therapist's ability to experience the countertransference feelings, rather than expressing or acting on them, and to use the feelings that were evoked to understand the client's inner world.

The totalistic perspective

The totalistic perspective views countertransference as all of the therapist's reactions to the client. According to this perspective, the therapist's unconscious understands the client in a way that the conscious cannot, and the therapist's countertransference reactions provide a mirror to the inner world of the client. Hence, countertransference can be used as a tool to understand the client.

Heimann (1950) also noted that not all reactions of the client are transference, rather some are realistic reactions to the therapist. It is important to differentiate these, and also to understand which countertransference feelings are informative about the client and those that are more to do with the therapist. Finally, Heimann believed that it was important for therapists to reflect on and give meaning to their countertransference feelings but she did not think that it was appropriate to share these with clients, as to do so could create a burden for clients and distract them from the therapy.

Heimann's (1950) paper is regarded as seminal and appears to signify the beginning of a shift in attitudes and beliefs about countertransference – a turning of the tide from countertransference as an impediment to therapy to countertransference as a valuable therapeutic tool, a way of understanding and knowing something about the client that is otherwise unavailable to the therapist's conscious mind.

At a similar time, and within the totalistic tradition, Winnicott (1949), also an object relations theorist, wrote about intense emotional responses he had experienced in relation to severely disturbed patients. In his paper titled 'Hate in the Counter-Transference', Winnicott differentiated between what he termed subjective and objective countertransference. He used the term **subjective countertransference** to describe those aspects of the countertransference reaction that originated in the therapist's personal unresolved issues. Winnicott used the term **objective countertransference**, on the other hand, to refer to those aspects of the countertransference that were a realistic response to the personality and behaviour of the client.

Winnicott (1949) proposed that the objective aspect of countertransference, including the emotions of love and hate, were the results of the 'crude feelings imputed (by the client) to (the therapist)' and that these emerged from the patient's history of disturbed formative relationships and their object representations (p. 70).

As will be discussed later in more depth, some argue that it is important for therapists to reflect on both aspects of countertransference reactions – those that relate to our own formative experiences of relationships and our own unresolved issues, as well as those aspects of countertransference that are a realistic response to the challenging or triggering behaviours of the client (e.g., Kiesler, 2001; Shafranske & Falender, 2008). These concepts will be further explored throughout the book.

Objective and subjective countertransference

Winnicott (1949) introduced the idea of objective and subjective aspects of countertransference. Objective aspects refer to those reactions that are a response to the personality and behaviour of the client in therapy, and the emotions that the client attributes to the therapist. Subjective aspects emanate from the therapist's own personal issues and sensitivities. Many countertransference reactions may have both objective and subjective aspects.

In 1957, Racker, also writing within the totalistic perspective, reflected on the lack of systematic thought that had been given to countertransference in the previous 40 years and commended the shift that was occurring towards greater attention to countertransference. In line with Heimann, Racker (1957) argued that this lack of attention had been due to analysts' previous emphasis on the ideal of objectivity, which led to the blocking of their own subjectivity and the rejection of their countertransference emotions. Racker argued that the analyst's capacity to understand the transference depended upon acceptance of his own countertransference and recognition of his identification with the patient's internal objects (or internal representations of others). Importantly, Racker (1957) reminded analysts that there are two personalities in therapy:

> The first distortion of truth in 'the myth of the analytic situation' is that analysis is an interaction between a sick person and a healthy one. The truth is that it is an interaction between two personalities ... each personality has its internal and external dependencies, anxieties and pathological defenses; each is also a child with his internal parents; and each of these whole personalities – that of the analysand and that of the analyst – responds to every event of the analytic situation. (p. 308–309)

In doing so, Racker foreshadowed the development of interpersonal and relational approaches to countertransference with his emphasis on the presence of the two subjectivities of therapist and client in relationship with each other.

Racker (1957) also introduced further aspects or types of countertransference reactions. According to Racker, in the process of attending to and experiencing empathy for the client, the analyst may identify with the client. He used the terms **complementary and concordant countertransference**. According to Racker (1957), concordant countertransference occurred when a therapist identified with a client's ego, id, or superego, and a complementary countertransference resulted from an identification with a client's internalised object (or object representation).

Concordant and complementary countertransference

Currently, concordant countertransference can be understood as the therapist's identification with a client's self-representation.

Complementary countertransference can be understood as the therapist's identification with a client's object or other representation.

The totalistic perspective of countertransference and the concepts of objective and subjective countertransference, and concordant and complementary countertransference, are still relevant and used by many therapists. The totalistic perspective is also used in research in which therapists or trainee therapists are asked to report on or write about their countertransference reactions (e.g., Betan, Heim, Conklin, & Westen, 2005; Cartwright, Rhodes, King, & Shires, 2014). The totalistic perspective heralded a shift to what has been termed a two-person psychology.

Relational perspectives

Relational approaches emphasise a two-person psychology in contrast to classical psychoanalysis, which has been critiqued as being a one-person psychology. According to relational theorists (Aron, 1990; Mitchell, 1998), the emphasis in

Freud's drive theory was on the intrapsychic world of the client rather than on the interpersonal world, and transference was conceptualised as occurring in the mind of the client rather than occurring in the interaction between therapist and client. Classical psychoanalysis emphasised drive theory, while relational perspectives emphasise the central importance of relationships both developmentally and in therapy. Relational perspectives, similar to object relations theory and attachment theory, view psychopathologies as originating in significant formative relationships, which lead to the development of an individual's pattern of interpersonal relatedness and their inner representations of these relationships (Aron, 1990). An aim of therapy is for the client to gain understanding of his interpersonal patterns of relating in therapy, which will in turn support the development of self-awareness and facilitate more satisfying relationships and psychological wellbeing, both in therapy and in everyday life (Lotterman, 2014). In practice, relational approaches focus on the here and now. The therapist and client are seen as co-participants who mutually influence each other, and engage in and collaboratively explore, in an ongoing way, the therapist's and client's contributions to interactions (Safran & Kraus, 2014).

In regard to countertransference, the shift to a two-person psychology and relational perspectives continued to challenge the classical notion (as did totalistic perspectives) that it was desirable or even possible for the therapist to stand outside the therapeutic process (Safran & Muran, 2000). Instead relational perspectives place importance on exploring the subjectivity of both the client and the therapist within the therapeutic relationship as it evolves (Lotterman, 2014), and countertransference is seen as co-constructed with contributions from both therapist and client (Gabbard, 2001). Each therapeutic relationship is regarded as unique because of the unique combination of the two personalities and what each brings to the relationship.

In therapeutic interactions, it is seen as desirable that the therapist allows herself to be 'immersed' or become 'embedded in the relational matrix' of the client, experience the countertransference fully, and then 'dis-embed' in order to consider how the therapist can help the client expand their relational con figuration and move the therapy forward (Safran, 2002, pp. 191–192). Hence, the relational perspectives of countertransference also see countertransference as providing insight into client's relational patterns, as well as placing emphasis on the co-construction of countertransference by the therapist and client contributions.

Gelso and Hayes' view of countertransference

Finally, it is important to acknowledge Gelso's and Hayes' (Gelso & Hayes, 2007; Hayes, 1995) psychodynamic perspective on countertransference, which they describe as integrative. These authors are leading countertransference researchers and some of their work is discussed in Chapters 2 and 6. Gelso and

Hayes view countertransference as the therapist's reactions, both internal and external, that are shaped by the therapist's past and also present unresolved conflicts and vulnerabilities. The trigger for countertransference is often behaviours of the client but can also be aspects of the therapeutic situation. While they acknowledge that clients evoke reactions in therapists, they argue that we should only consider a therapist reaction to be countertransference if the therapist's unresolved issues or vulnerabilities are triggered. In doing so, they put emphasis on what has been termed subjective countertransference.

Hayes (1995) also developed a conceptual model of countertransference, in order to support research in this area. According to this model, countertransference consists of five components: the origins, triggers, manifestations, effects and management. In Chapter 6 we will discuss a study into trainee psychologists' experiences of these five components and consider a method of reflective practice based on this conceptual model.

Explaining countertransference from psychodynamic perspectives

Before turning to integrative psychotherapy and CBT perspectives of countertransference, it is important to consider the theories that have been developed by psychoanalysts and psychodynamic therapists to explain the processes that underlie countertransference. We will examine three of these – projective identification, role responsivity, and complementarity.

Countertransference: Projective identification, role responsivity, or interpersonal complementarity

Projective identification: The therapist identifies with a self- or other-representation that is projected by the client onto or into them and experiences the associated emotions.

Role responsivity: The client takes up a role in relation to the therapist and the therapist accepts a complementary role. Countertransference reactions occur as part of the therapist's role-responsivity.

Interpersonal complementarity: Therapists respond to the maladaptive interpersonal style of the client in a complementary way. Clients pull for reactions in therapists and therapists in turn are hooked into a complementary way of responding.

Projective identification

The concept of projective identification is often viewed as an explanation for countertransference. Melanie Klein, who is regarded as the primary founder of object relations theory, introduced the idea of projective identification in 1946 in relation to her theory of infant development (Klein, 1946). Klein viewed projective identification as a phantasy in which the infant's unwanted or bad aspects of self were split off and projected into the mother in order to control and possess her. Good aspects of the self were also projected into the mother and this could allow for development of the ego and positive self–object relations.

Klein did not link projective identification with countertransference. However, the concept of projective identification has been taken up by some psychodynamic therapists as a valuable explanation for the processes of transference and counter-transference. While there is debate about what constitutes projective identification, Gabbard (2017) provides an overview of what he sees as a current and common understanding of projective identification. This includes three steps:

- Step One – a client disavows and projects a self or object (other) representation 'placing it into' the therapist (p. 159). This projection of the disavowed aspect of self is accompanied by the emotional content associated with the unwanted self or object representation.
- Step Two – the client exerts interpersonal pressure on the therapist and 'nudges' the therapist to experience or identify with the projected aspect of self or other, including the experience of the emotional content (p. 160).
- Step Three – ideally the therapist is able to experience and contain the emotion associated with the disavowed and projected aspects of the client's self, which makes it possible for the client to take back, perhaps in a different form, that which was projected (p. 160).

According to Gabbard (2017), the first step is the transference and the second step the countertransference. The third step can be viewed as the process by which the therapist contains their countertransference reaction and under-stands its meaning for the client. Gabbard observes that these reactions can be so powerful that therapists often need to work through their reactions between sessions when they are no longer under the direct influence of the projections. The strength of the reaction may also depend on the hook in the therapist's personality. We vary in relation to what hooks us and what does not.

Role responsivity

Sandler (1976) introduced another way of thinking about the dynamics under-lying transference and countertransference. Sandler wrote that he did not find the concepts of projection and projective identification useful in understanding

---

Pause and reflect: Projective identification

When therapists talk about projective identification, they often talk about experiencing powerful emotional reactions and feeling as if they are not themselves, or they feel they have been taken over by the emotions, and/or are not able to think properly.

Have you experienced that sense of not being like yourself in therapy?

Does thinking about the notion of projective identification make sense for you in reflecting back on that time? Or do you have an alternative explanation?

---

the processes of transference and countertransference. Rather he attempted to make sense of the unconscious dynamics through the consideration of what he referred to as intrapsychic role relationships. According to Sandler, the client puts himself into a particular role at any moment in time in therapy and the therapist reflexively accepts a complementary role. The roles that the client takes are influenced by the client's self and object (other) representations along their needs and defences. Sandler discusses therapists' tendencies to see their responses as irrational rather than considering these reactions as their role responsiveness. Rather he recommended that the therapists recognise countertransference reactions as their role responsiveness and work to understand the role relationships that the client is enacting.

Pause and reflect: Role adoption

Can you think back to a time, either during your own therapy or perhaps in clinical supervision that you may have put yourself in a role in relation to your therapist or supervisor? Thinking back on that, what was the role and what do you think underlay your adoption of this role?

Interpersonal complementarity

Kiesler's (2001) approach to countertransference uses language that is accessible to psychoanalytic therapists and those from other therapeutic approaches. Kiesler's (1983) interpersonal perspective emerged from his interest in applying interpersonal communication theory to psychotherapy practice and from his research into what he called interpersonal complementarity. Kiesler's (1983, 2001) approach assumes that individuals encounter problems in relationships because of their problematic interpersonal styles, which evoke counter-communications from others including those who are important or significant in their lives. In therapy, the therapist registers the impact messages from the client and responds in a complementary way (Kiesler, 2001). Therapists are then hooked into the client's maladaptive pattern of interpersonal relationships.

According to Kiesler (2001), the therapist's complementary response is the objective countertransference. These complementary responses evoked by the client will be similar to responses of others to the client in his daily life. Subjective countertransference, on the other hand, refers to reactions to the client that originate in the unresolved issues of the therapist. Kiesler (2001) argued that it is useful for therapists to consider deviations from the baseline in their reactions to clients when differentiating between the subjective and objective aspects of countertransference, and to also note when their reactions are different from those of other colleagues or supervisors, which could indicate a subjective countertransference.

Countertransference in integrative approaches

There has been a movement in recent years towards psychotherapy integration. Many therapists, if asked, describe themselves as integrative or eclectic (Norcross, Karpiak, & Lister, 2005). This movement towards integrative approaches appears to have emerged from a proliferation of therapeutic approaches, therapists gaining training and experience in a range of approaches, and research evidence that suggests that no therapeutic approach is superior to others (Norcross et al., 2005). This movement has run parallel to the search for common factors – the core features of psychotherapy approaches that are associated with positive therapy outcomes.

Integrative approaches place emphasis on therapeutic strategies related to the therapeutic relationship and the therapeutic alliance (Erskine, 2015). Integrative psychotherapists tend to hold the view that the therapeutic relationship, while not sufficient for change, is a curative factor in and of itself (Halgin & McEntee, 2013). From this perspective, creating a climate of empathy and acceptance can provide the client with increased self-worth and self-acceptance and contribute to changing clients' dysfunctional thoughts, emotions, and behaviours towards self and other (Gold, 2013).

As part of this attention to the therapeutic relationship, integrative therapists also attend to transference and countertransference (e.g., Erskine, 2015; Gold & Wachtel, 2013; Stricker & Gold, 2013). Gold and Wachtel (2013), for example, view transference reactions as manifestations of ways of thinking about and representing self and other, although they note that sometimes client's reactions to therapists reflect the therapist's behaviours or attitudes rather than transference. Countertransference is conceptualised as the therapist's reactions to the client which are a blend of the feelings, thoughts, and behaviours evoked by the client and also the therapist's own character and personal history (Gold & Wachtel, 2013). Transference and countertransference and the therapeutic interaction are viewed as providing crucial data for understanding the client and therapist, and for bringing about change.

Halgin and McIntee (2013) also discuss the challenges that integrative psychotherapists and clients face in regard to shifts in therapeutic techniques, which can be characteristic of integrative approaches. They observe that a therapist shifting, for example, from a psychodynamic exploratory approach to educative and directive techniques in the same session may be challenging for a client and evoke transference reactions. They also argue that therapists have to be aware of how their countertransference reactions might influence their choice of interventions; for example, a therapist who is uncomfortable with emotional intensity may unconsciously shift to using a more skills-based intervention to avoid the client's emotions. As with other therapeutic approaches, integrative psychotherapists also place emphasis on being aware of countertransference reactions and responding constructively in ways that assist the client to develop new ways of understanding themselves and others (Stricker & Gold, 2013).

Countertransference in cognitive-behavioural therapy

There has been much less discussion of countertransference in cognitive therapy (CT) and cognitive-behavioural therapy (CBT) compared to psychodynamic and integrative approaches. This is not surprising given that the concepts of transference and countertransference originated within and are central to psychoanalytic/psychodynamic paradigms. The transference–countertransference relationship can also be viewed as an aspect of the therapeutic relationship. CBT therapists generally have placed less emphasis on the therapeutic relationship (Cartwright, 2011; Gilbert & Leahy, 2007). While a good collaborative relationship is viewed as important in CBT, this relationship is seen as necessary in providing the underpinning for the CBT interventions that are seen as key to positive therapy outcomes. Despite this, there appears to be increasing interest in the therapeutic relationship and in transference and countertransference in CBT, although these terms may have different meanings to a CBT therapist as they will be understood within a CBT framework.

Beck, the founder of CT, along with his colleagues Freeman and Davis (2004) discussed transference and countertransference in their text on cognitive therapy for personality disorders. They note that 'both patient and therapist are likely to experience strong emotional reactions to one another' during treatment for a personality disorder (p. 108). While they acknowledge that these reactions have been traditionally referred to as transference and countertransference, they argue that it works better within a CT framework to refer to these client and therapist reactions as 'emotional reactions' (2004, p. 108).

Transference, they argue, can be understood in CT terms as resulting from individuals' overgeneralised beliefs, expectations, and assumptions about relationships that have been learnt through life experiences (Beck et al., 2004). Interestingly, Beck and colleagues argue that the client's emotional reactions to the therapist and therapy processes are potential sources of information about the client's thoughts and beliefs and are 'windows into the patient's private world' (p. 108), echoing the writings of Heimann (1950) and other psychodynamic therapists. The authors also talk about the importance of the therapist being attuned to her own countertransference reactions – the emotions, physical sensations, shifts in mood, and thoughts about the client or therapy events. They recommend that therapists use thought records or cognitive structuring techniques to help themselves manage their emotional reactions that might impact therapy. They also stress that it is important for therapists to maintain non-judgmental and sympathetic responses to clients and the problematic patterns with which clients struggle.

Newman (2013) in his book on core competencies in CBT also discusses transference as resulting from the client's 'overgeneralised interpersonal beliefs' that influence how he perceives and responds to the therapist. He refers to countertransference as the therapist's cognitive, emotional, and behavioural responses to the client, which may be 'normative' to the client – that is, may reflect a common response of others to the client. Hence, Beck and colleagues along with Newman are emphasising what psychodynamic therapists sometimes refer to as objective countertransference.

Robert Leahy (2007), on the other hand, emphasises the subjective aspects of countertransference – the impact of the therapist's own maladaptive schemas on their emotional and cognitive reactions to the client. He talks about the transference relationship as consisting of all of the personal and interpersonal processes that occur between client and therapist. These processes are influenced by the client's schemas about the self and about others. Leahy also addresses intrapsychic processes that can be at play (repression, denial) and the use of interpersonal strategies (clinging, stonewalling).

According to Leahy (2007), therapists also hold their own personal and interpersonal schemas that influence their reactions to different groups of clients. He outlines a number of different therapist schemas that can result in countertransference reactions. Examples include demanding standards, need for approval, and emotional inhibition. Therapists with demanding standards, for example, may believe that they should work effectively with all clients and that clients should also work at therapy and do well. Clients struggling with motivation or engaging in self-defeating behaviours are likely to evoke countertransference reactions in therapists who have demanding standards.

Therapists who believe they need approval may feel that they are not doing well as therapists if clients are annoyed with them. They may also avoid touching on sensitive or challenging topics that might lead to client disapproval. Importantly, Leahy (2007) addresses issues related to therapists' emotional philosophies – beliefs around the importance of emotions and whether they should be avoided, paid attention to, or deepened. Therapists who view emotions as distracting or indulgent may have negative or avoidant reactions to clients' emotions and communicate a critical attitude or lack of empathy to client emotional reactions, which can then reinforce clients' problematic self and other schemas (Leahy, 2007).

Hence, CBT perspectives of transference emphasise the central role of cognitions – of client's overgeneralised beliefs or schemas that have developed from formative relationships and which influence the way that the client feels, thinks, and behaves in therapy towards the therapy and therapy processes. Countertransference, on the other hand, is influenced by the beliefs or schemas of the therapist that are triggered by clients' behaviours and therapy events. These beliefs and schemas can be therapy-interfering and can reinforce a client's overgeneralised personal and interpersonal schemas. Viewed from these perspectives, countertransference reactions can be helpful in that they alert the client to potential transferences (or activation of interpersonal schemas) of the client or can also be problematic if they represent the schemas of the therapist.

Definition of countertransference used in this book

The perspective of CT used in this text is influenced by a number of the perspectives discussed above, including the totalistic, relational, complementary, and integrative perspectives. Throughout the book, CT will be conceptualised as the emotional, cognitive, and bodily reactions of the therapist to the client or the therapy situation and context. Countertransference reactions can lead to countertransference behaviours that can have negative effects on clients and on therapeutic relationships.

Different aspects of countertransference are considered within this conceptualisation. These include the reactions that are evoked or provoked by the client or therapy context and are informative of the client's experiences in therapy (objective countertransference), and those reactions that originate in the therapist's unresolved personal issues, sensitivities, or vulnerabilities (subjective countertransference). It is acknowledged that many countertransference reactions will include both aspects of countertransference. Not all reactions of the therapist, however, are considered countertransference. Some reactions may reflect a mature response of the therapist to the client's experiences or situation (for example, sadness for a client who has experienced a loss, or a feeling of happiness for a client who has finally reached a long-term goal). Hence, it differs in this aspect from the totalistic perspective.

As well as considering the potential for the negative effects of CT behaviours, the approach used throughout regards countertransference as a potential and valuable source of insight into the client's inner world. This is in line with psychodynamic conceptualisations and the results of CT research that indicate that CT behaviours can have negative effects on therapy outcomes while understanding and managing CT can enhance therapy outcomes (Hayes, Gelso,

Goldberg, & Kivlighan, 2018). The main focus of the approach to countertransference that is introduced in Chapter 3 is on conceptualising or making sense of our countertransference reactions and then managing these in ways that are likely to enhance rather than detract from therapeutic relationships and therapy outcomes.

Case study: Jack and Carl

Jack, 24 years old, was referred by his general practitioner for depression and anxiety. Jack expressed some ambivalence about seeing a therapist but after the first session with his therapist Carl (28 years old), Jack said that he would like some help and that he feels like he is not making anything of himself and wants to 'get his act together'.

Jack tells his therapist that his father had been a successful sportsman and Jack 'really looked up to him' during his childhood and still does. However, his father was also 'pretty frightening' when he was 'in a bad mood' and then he would be verbally critical of Jack. Jack began getting into fights at school when he was about 12 and his school work deteriorated. This enraged his father who would shake him and tell him he was a little piece of shit, f-ing useless, a hopeless case, and an embarrassment. Later, Jack says he now gets on well with his father as long as they don't talk about his work at McDonald's or his future.

The therapist feels empathic towards Jack and feels angry towards the father as he listens to Jack talk about him. At one point, Carl has an image of Carl's own father shouting at him and insulting him when he was 10 years old and this increases his empathy for Jack.

It's the fourth session and Jack often relates to the therapist in a matey way – being friendly and chatty when he gets the opportunity. The therapist, Carl, finds himself enjoying this and looks forward to seeing the client. He feels he is a good match for the client. However, the supervisor has given him feedback that the sessions are a bit superficial and that Carl could focus more on the client's experiences of his father and the impact of these experiences on his views of himself and of others. The supervisor reminds Carl that Jack has described being quite depressed although this is not evident in sessions.

During the next session, Carl does a timeline with Jack and Jack looks sad as he relates some of the events with his father in early adolescence. Carl once again has an image of his father shouting at him and says to Jack how upsetting that must have been for him as a child – hearing those critical statements from his father. Jack gets tears in his eyes, and then changes quite quickly, sitting up in his chair and saying that he doesn't want to 'be a wuss who is obsessed with the past like therapists are'. He looks at Carl then quickly looks away. Carl experiences a flash of anger at Jack and then feels guilty as Carl now looks crestfallen.

Pause and reflect: Carl and Jack

1. Which of Carl's reactions might be considered countertransference?
2. Which aspects of Carl's reactions might be related to his own personal issues and sensitivities?
3. Which of Carl's reactions might be evoked, at least in part, by the client?
4. How might Carl unwittingly engage in countertransference behaviours?

Summary

This chapter presented an historical overview of the development of the concept of countertransference, beginning with Freud's classical view, followed by the totalistic perspective and related concepts, the relational perspective, and the integrative perspective of Hayes and Gelso. We also considered three explanations for the interpersonal processes that underlie countertransference – projective identification, role responsivity, and interpersonal complementarity.

We then considered integrative psychotherapy and CBT perspectives. Integrative therapists share similar understandings of countertransference as psychodynamic therapists. There is also increasing interest in countertransference in CBT approaches, although countertransference is sometimes simply referred to as therapist emotions in order to be consistent within a CBT framework.

Recommended readings

Cartwright, C. (2011). Transference, countertransference, and reflective practice in cognitive therapy. *Clinical Psychologist, 15,* 112–120.

Gabbard, G. (2001). A contemporary psychoanalytic model of countertransference. *Journal of Clinical Psychology, 57,* 983–991.

Gabbard, G. (2017). *Long-term psychodynamic psychotherapy: A basic text.* Arlington, VA: American Psychiatric Association.

Hayes, J. A., Gelso, C. J., Goldberg, S., & Kivlighan, D. M. (2018). Countertransference management and effective psychotherapy: Meta-analytic findings. *Psychotherapy, 55,* 496–512.

Kiesler, D. (2001). Therapist countertransference: In search of common themes and empirical referents. *Psychotherapy in Practice, 57,* 1053–1063.

2

Countertransference and the Therapeutic Relationship

This chapter considers the therapeutic relationship and its components – the real relationship, the working alliance, and the transference–countertransference relationship – and the influence that countertransference has on the therapeutic relationship. In order to assist therapists to be mindful and to recognise their own subjective responses to clients, it briefly examines the types of countertransference reactions that therapists and trainees experience in their therapeutic work, and the types of reactions that experienced therapists/supervisors view as characteristic of countertransference. The chapter then discusses different aspects of countertransference – positive and negative countertransference, and subjective and objective countertransference. We then turn to the question of cultural countertransference that arises in cross-cultural therapeutic relationships in which therapist and client are of different cultural background. The chapter ends with a brief discussion of the relationship between countertransference and professional and ethical issues.

The real relationship, the therapeutic alliance, and the transference–countertransference relationship

Gelso and Carter (1985) were the first to offer a definition of the therapeutic relationship as 'the feelings and attitudes that (therapist and client) have toward one another, and the manner in which these are expressed' (p. 159). A tripartite model of the therapeutic relationship has developed over recent decades (Gelso,

2014). According to this model, the therapeutic relationship can be viewed as having three components – a real relationship, a working or therapeutic alliance, and the transference and countertransference relationship. At any moment in a therapy session, one component may be more salient than the other two components and the salience of the different components will shift within therapy sessions and across time. Each component influences the other components. For example, therapeutic disruptions related to transference and/or countertransference issues that emerge in a therapy session, or across a series of therapy sessions, are likely to impact the therapeutic alliance and the therapist and client's abilities to work collaboratively together.

The real relationship

The term real relationship is most often used to refer to the personal relationship that develops between the therapist and client, which is genuine and contains realistic perceptions and experiences of the other (Gelso, 2014; Greenson & Wexler, 1969). This real relationship can also be thought of as providing the foundations for the therapeutic relationship (Gelso, 2014).

Pause and reflect: Carl and Jack

Thinking back on Carl (therapist) and Jack (client), can you see any evidence of a 'real' relationship between the two? And if so, what is the quality of this 'real' relationship?

The working alliance

The therapeutic or working alliance has been the focus of much research over the recent decades. In 1979, Bordin proposed that a strong working alliance is characterised by three conditions – a working bond between therapist and client, agreement on the goals of therapy, and agreement on the tasks that will be undertaken to reach these goals. A number of meta-analytic reviews of studies have examined the relationship between the working alliance and therapy outcomes (e.g., Flückiger, Del Re, Wampold, & Horvath, 2018; Martin, Garske, & Davis, 2000) and found a robust and positive relationship, which is consistent across outcomes measures, assessors, treatment approaches, and countries.

The transference–countertransference relationship

The third component of the therapeutic relationship is the transference and countertransference relationship or configuration (Gelso, 2014). Research into the working alliance has been much more extensive than research into countertransference and its association with therapy outcomes. However, there have now been two meta-analytic studies of countertransference (Hayes, Gelso, & Hummel, 2011; Hayes et al., 2018). In the most recent meta-analysis, the researchers reviewed all studies that had examined the relationship between CT reactions or CT management and therapy outcomes. They found that the majority of these studies looked at what they referred to as immediate or proximate therapy outcomes rather than distal outcomes (Hayes et al., 2018). They reported on three analyses. The first analysis examined results from 14 studies and found an association between more frequent CT reactions and poorer therapy outcomes. While the association was relatively small, it was reliable across the studies. The second analysis of 13 studies found that better CT management was associated with fewer CT reactions. The third analysis included nine studies that had examined the relationship between CT management and therapy outcomes. The effect size was significant and of a large–medium effect size. Hence, the results suggest that CT reactions can have negative impacts on therapy outcomes and alternatively managing CT can have positive effects on therapy outcomes. These meta-analytic results support the views of psychodynamic therapists who have for many years argued that countertransference can have negative effects on the therapeutic relationship and therapy outcomes, while understanding and managing countertransference can enhance therapeutic relationships and outcomes.

Types of countertransference reactions

Countertransference manifests in feelings, thoughts and imagery, physiological or bodily reactions, and in urges and behaviours. A qualitative study conducted by colleagues and myself with 65 Australian and New Zealand clinical psychology trainees found that the trainees described a range of countertransference reactions in their client work (Cartwright et al., 2014). Trainees were asked to write about a recent countertransference reaction and to provide context in terms of what was happening in the session and how the client was responding to them or the therapy situation. Trainees reported six main types of countertransference reactions:

1. Wanting to protect or take care of
2. Empathising and identifying with the client
3. Feeling controlled, intimidated, or criticised
4. Feeling helpless or inadequate
5. Feeling overwhelmed, out of control, or immobilised
6. Feeling disengaged

The most common type of reaction described by trainees was *Wanting to protect or take care of* the client with whom they were working. Trainees described feelings of sadness, concern, or worry about a client and a desire to protect or take care of them. These reactions were often triggered by witnessing the client's distress or by hearing about the difficult or traumatic events or relationships they had experienced. Sometimes trainees reflected that they had engaged in countertransference behaviours, such as trying to 'fix' the client, or by rescuing the client by not challenging or extending the client in sessions.

The second theme was *Empathising and identifying with the client* (Cartwright et al., 2014). Trainees who described this type of countertransference reaction reported strong empathic responses to clients and found themselves identifying with the client. These reactions included strong feelings of sadness for clients who experienced significant loss, or identifying with a client's problems or concerns (such as worries about weight or appearance). On a small number of occasions, trainees felt it was hard to separate out what was theirs and what were the clients' feelings and concerns. At times this led to countertransference behaviours, for example, one trainee wrote that she realised later that she did not complete a full assessment with her client because she identified with the client's problems and normalised or minimised them internally.

The third type of countertransference reactions was titled *Feeling controlled, intimidated or criticised* (Cartwright et al., 2014). Trainees appeared to experience this reaction to clients who were being controlling or acting in critical or superior ways towards them. Trainees who described this type of countertransference reaction saw themselves as inadequate as therapists and sometimes dreaded sessions.

The fourth type of reaction was *Feeling helpless or inadequate* and this tended to occur with clients who were not progressing or who had difficulty setting goals or working towards them – clients who themselves may have been struggling with feelings of helplessness (Cartwright et al., 2014). These trainees also felt inadequate as therapists and tended to blame themselves for the client's lack of progress. Some thought these feelings of helplessness or inadequacy undermined their effectiveness with the clients.

A fifth type of reaction included *Feeling overwhelmed, out of control, or immobilised* and these reactions appeared to be in response to clients who were emotionally distressed, describing strong emotional states including anger, or had multiple problems that felt overwhelming to both the therapist and client (Cartwright et al., 2014).

In the final theme, *Feeling disengaged*, trainees described having difficulty connecting to or feeling disengaged from clients who appeared to be intellectualising or who were themselves lacking in emotional expression (Cartwright et al., 2014).

It is interesting to compare these countertransference reactions of trainees to the countertransference reactions of a group of experienced therapists who took part in a countertransference study (Betan et al., 2005). In this therapist study, 181 psychiatrists and clinical psychologists completed a number of measures including a countertransference questionnaire in regard to one randomly selected client (the last adult client seen in the previous week). The methods used in the two studies were different. The study with trainees (Cartwright et al., 2014) collected qualitative data and Betan and colleagues used a measure of countertransference – the Countertransference Questionnaire.

The experienced therapists reported eight main types of countertransference reactions. These included: overwhelmed/disorganised; helpless/inadequate; positive; special/overinvolved; sexualised; disengaged; parental/protective; and criticised/mistreated. As can be seen, a number of these overlap with the countertransference described by trainees. Trainees did not, however, describe any sexualised countertransference reactions. This may reflect a lack of such experience amongst the group of trainees but may also reflect discomfort with writing or talking about sexual feelings in a therapy situation. It has also been my experience in doing the training that it is rare for trainees to talk about sexualised experiences although this has sometimes occurred. Trainees may be cautious about talking about their personal reactions as they fear that they might be judged by their supervisors or trainers. On the other hand, having clients fall in love with you or having sexual feelings towards a client is something that all therapists are likely to experience at some point and hence we will return to this topic in Chapter 6, once we have developed a greater depth of understanding about transference and countertransference.

Distinguishing countertransference

An interesting study with experienced therapists who were also experienced clinical supervisors found a high level of agreement about the types of therapist reactions that are seen as manifestations of countertransference and those therapist reactions that are not. Forty-five experienced psychologists who had also acted as clinical supervisors for 10 years took part in a study of countertransference prototypes in order to examine the degree of consensus around countertransference manifestations (Hofsess & Tracey, 2010). The psychologists completed an online survey in which they were asked to rate the extent to which each of 108 items were likely to be manifestations of countertransference. The authors found that there was a high level of agreement among the therapists as to which items were prototypical of countertransference manifestations. Examples of highly rated items included: acts flirtatious with a client, loves a client, daydreams about relationships or events related to a client, loses all neutrality and sides with a client, rejects the client in session, engages in too much self-disclosure, and expresses hostility toward or about a client. Items which were not viewed as examples of countertransference included: expresses empathy for a client's loss, is comfortable in the presence of strong affect from a client, is prepared for supervision, feels confident working with most clients, is supportive, is emotionally in tune with a client, looks up literature related to a client's problems, and understands the influence of culture in a client's life. This study may be worth looking at in more depth as it will give you an understanding of a range of reactions that are seen, by experienced therapists, as prototypical of countertransference and those that are not.

Positive and negative countertransference

As will be seen from above, countertransference reactions can have a positive valence (feeling warm and protective, identifying empathically with a client) or a negative valence (feeling frustrated and critical or disengaged from a client). These can be thought about as positive and negative countertransference. It is important though to remember that both positive and negative countertransference reactions can be problematic if they are not understood and managed.

Positive countertransference tends to feel good or comfortable to the therapist and in my experience can be somewhat seductive or enticing; that is, the therapist can experience the positive feelings as congruent, enjoy them, and not question these reactions. A positive countertransference is likely to be made up of positive emotions and also complementary thoughts. For example, a client who is idealising a therapist may evoke thoughts such as, 'I'm doing really well with the client. We are such a good match. I think I am the right person for her. I will be able to help her move to a much better place in her life'.

It can feel pleasing or positive to be looked up to, to be idealised, or needed by a client – especially perhaps when we are in training and feeling uncertain about our own competencies as a therapist; or when we are working with many challenging clients. Feeling looked up to and needed by a client can also be personally comforting during difficult times in our lives and it might be easier to simply go with these feelings rather than to question what they mean for the client and the therapy plan. In accepting these thoughts and feeling unquestioningly, the therapist can miss what is really happening for the client. For example, a therapist may not perceive the problematic aspects of a client's idealisation of the therapist and the client's patterns of relating to others that underlie this idealisation. Positive countertransference reactions can also lead to rescue attempts, to avoiding the challenging of clients or not using interventions that might stretch them. These feelings can also impact our assessment and conceptualisation of the client's problems as we minimise them.

In terms of negative countertransference, a client who is being critical of a therapist is likely to evoke feelings of hurt, anger, frustration, or desire to withdraw and/or perhaps a sense of incompetence and feeling critical of oneself as well as the client. These emotional reactions are likely to be associated with negative thoughts which could include 'I've tried my best with this client. The client is just ungrateful and not willing to change. The client doesn't want to get better. He's quite a nasty person and I'm not good enough to be able to help this client'. As we will discuss more in the next chapter, these thoughts and feelings are important and tell us something about the client's experiences and also that of the therapist. It may be, for example, that the client is feeling some of these feelings as well – hurt, anger, frustration or the desire to withdraw – or it may be that the client is acting towards the therapist as his caregiver/s acted towards him.

Objective and subjective countertransference

As noted earlier, these terms are used through this text as they provide a useful way for thinking about different aspects of our countertransference reactions. Objective countertransference is used to refer to those aspects of our counter-transference reactions that are evoked, provoked, induced or pulled for by the client's behaviour and the therapy situation. Subjective (or personal) countertrans-ference refers to those aspects of the therapist's countertransference that originate in the client's sensitivities or unresolved issues. Subjective countertransference can also be thought of as the therapist's transference to the client, in which the therapist's relationships with significant others in the past influence the thera-pist's reaction to the client's behaviour and the problems they are discussing.

It seems likely that many countertransference reactions contain elements of both subjective and objective countertransference. For example, a therapist may react with hurt and then anger at a client who expresses dissatisfaction with the therapist. The client may have experienced a failure of care and responsivity during childhood and is now experiencing the therapist as uncar-ing and unresponsive. The therapist feels himself trapped in being uncaring and unresponsive for no matter how hard he tries to relate to and engage with the client, the client still sees him in this way. The client's behaviour towards the therapist also triggers a personal countertransference reaction for the ther-apist. The therapist has often felt hurt and then angry with his father whom he felt treated him as being a disappointment throughout his childhood and these feelings are now triggered in the current situation with his client.

As you can see from the above example, it is important for the therapist to be able to separate out and understand each of these aspects of the countertransference – the objective and realistic reaction to the client's criticisms, and the therapist's personal or subjective reactions to the client's criticism. I place emphasis on understanding both of these aspects of countertransference, and how they can interact, throughout this text.

Understanding your personal countertransference reactions

Training programmes often emphasise the need for trainees to have therapy for themselves. Being a client is helpful for understanding the client's posi-tion in the therapeutic relationship and the vulnerability of this position.

Personal experience of therapy can help us to understand the challenges clients face in being open about very personal experiences and the coping strategies (or defences) that clients use when they are feeling challenged or vulnerable. It is also helpful to experience different types of therapist behaviours such as empathic responses, validation, challenge, and managing a therapeutic disruption. Another advantage of having one's own therapy is that it helps us to have greater understanding of our own formative experiences and how these have impacted our experiences of self, of others, and of relationships. Therapy helps us to become aware of our own templates for relationships that contribute to our countertransference reactions.

Robert Leahy (2007) has written about the effects of schematic mismatches that can occur in therapeutic relationships. According to this perspective, common problems in the therapeutic relationship can emerge from the schemas (or core beliefs) that clients and therapists bring to therapy situations that can lead to transference and countertransference reactions and create disruptions within therapeutic relationships. As discussed in Chapter 1, Leahy (2007) outlines a number of therapist schemas that he believes underlie countertransference reactions to clients. These therapist schemas influence our responses to clients and the clients we find challenging or alternatively with whom we feel comfortable working. As Leahy points out, it is a good idea for therapists to take notice of which types of clients or client problems push our buttons, and alternatively those we find easier to work with, some of whom may hold schemas that may match our own.

Therapists with a schema of control and the belief that they must be in control of their lives, and what is around them, may experience negative countertransference reactions to clients who are disorganised and have a chaotic lifestyle. Therapists who need approval may find critical clients very difficult to work with and may avoid challenging clients generally in order to avoid disapproval.

Positive countertransference reactions on the other hand may be evoked by clients whose schemas match ours (Leahy, 2007). Therapists with demanding standards may feel admiring towards clients who are perfectionistic and expect themselves to achieve in whatever they do. These therapists may be at risk of missing the clients' emotional problems and struggles that underlie the perfectionist tendencies. Becoming aware of our own self and relational schemas will help us to understand and manage our countertransference reactions to clients.

Pause and reflect: Countertransference reaction

Have you noticed any types of client behaviour that appear to trigger you into a countertransference reaction? And if so, what is the schema that underlies your reaction?

Cultural countertransference

In this section of the chapter, we are going to first consider what is meant by cultural countertransference (and transference) and the influence of socio-cultural and historical contexts on these therapist and client reactions. We will then briefly consider the challenges of working competently cross-culturally when many therapists are trained in psychotherapies that reflect Western perspectives of what it is to be human.

In the book so far, we have considered the influence of clients' and therapists' formative experiences on the development of our views or representations of self, of others, and of relationships. Thinking about cultural countertransference draws our attention to wider cultural influences – both past and present – that impact our personal development, and our place in the world in relation to others. Currently, there is only a small amount of published research in the area of cultural countertransference, and as with countertransference generally there is not an established definition of cultural countertransference, although many authors have contributed to discussions in this area.

Most commonly, cultural countertransference is seen as countertransference arising in cross-cultural therapy when therapist and client are of different cultural or ethnic/racial backgrounds. However, cultural countertransference can arguably arise also when therapists and clients are of different sexual orientation, gender, religion, and even socioeconomic status (Gelso & Hayes, 2007). Gelso and Mohr (2001) talk about the culture-related distortions that therapists can have in regard to clients in cross-cultural therapy, and the problematic behaviours that can result from therapists' internalisation of negative cultural narratives related to minority groups.

Comas-Diaz and Jacobsen (1995) developed a model of ethnocultural transference and countertransference reactions that they observed occur in psychotherapy dyads of the same ethnicity and of different ethnicities. Comas-Diaz (2012), in her text on cultural competence, describes culture as the elephant in the therapy room and argues that cultural differences in the therapist–client dyad can evoke strong unconscious reactions in clients and therapists. Gelso and Mohr (2001) also suggest that the intensity of the therapeutic relationship generally pulls for cultural transference and countertransference. For therapists working cross-culturally, countertransference reactions can result in 'ethnocultural disorientation' and empathic stumbling (Comas-Diaz & Jacobsen, 1991, p. 392).

Christopher Bonovitz (2005), a psychoanalyst, further argues that therapy is a microcosm of the sociocultural contexts of therapists and clients. According to Bonovitz, our sociocultural history shapes our representations of self and other, and transference and countertransference can be thought of as 'embodying aspects of the historical relations between (the therapist and client's) respective cultures' expressed within the therapeutic relationship (Bonovitz, 2005, p. 63).

Cultural transference

Many individuals from minority groups experience social stigma as part of their everyday lives. Stigmatisation and the associated cultural narratives result in misunderstandings and discriminatory behaviour. Minority clients also rarely see themselves reflected back to themselves by their therapists (Comas-Diaz, 2012). It seems likely then that minority-group clients beginning therapy may be apprehensive about how mainstream therapists will view them and respond to them.

Comas-Diaz and Jacobsen (1995) refer to ethnocultural transference and countertransference that can arise in inter-ethnic therapy dyads. Comas-Diaz (2012) in her text on cultural competence outlines a number of transference reactions that ethnic minority clients experience working with non-minority therapists. These include overcompliance and friendliness towards therapists, denial of the relevance of culture and ethnicity to the therapy process, reactions of mistrust, suspicion or hostility to therapists whose motivations and ability to understand they distrust (because they are not from a minority culture), and finally, ambivalence in which clients become attached to therapists, on the other hand, but have trouble identifying with therapists and continue to doubt that majority culture therapists can ever really understand.

When there has been a history of oppression and especially when the impact of oppression and cultural prejudice still exists, then cultural transference and countertransference may be inevitable (Gelso & Mohr, 2001). In Britain, this would be relevant to a white therapist working with clients of African Caribbean descent; in Aotearoa New Zealand, a Pākehā therapist (of European descent) with Māori or Pasifika clients; in Australia, a First Nations client with a white Australian therapist; and a black African American or First Nations American working with a white therapist in the United States. Gelso and Mohr (2001) also remind us to be cautious about classifying a client's reaction to a therapist as cultural transference as minority clients' reactions to majority therapists are not necessarily transferential – but rather can also be realistic reactions to actual therapist behaviours and to ongoing social discrimination and stigmatisation.

Cultural countertransference

Comas-Diaz and Jacobsen (1995) in their cross-cultural work also observed a number of therapist countertransference reactions in inter-ethnic dyads. According to Comas-Diaz (2012), these include the denial or lack of recognition of ethnic or cultural differences, which results in cultural issues being unavailable for the client to talk about, therapists being overly curious about the client's cultural background, feelings of pity or guilt, which can be demobilising for the therapist and unhelpful for the client, and aggression towards clients who arouse feelings of guilt or awareness of privilege, and also ambivalence.

A small number of studies have also provided insights into cultural countertransference.

Studies of cross-cultural countertransference

Stampey (2008) interviewed 17 social workers in the United States about their experiences of working cross-culturally. Stampey concluded that key sources of countertransference reactions discussed by participants appeared to be beliefs that originated in participants' families of origin and also social influences including the media. Examples of countertransference included a participant expressing a lack of understanding of families who are not supportive of each other in times of difficulty, not understanding why a First Nations client kept talking about the loss of the tribe's land, and seeing a potential violent offender in every young male African American service user.

Tummala-Narra and colleagues (2018) interviewed 20 psychoanalytic psychologists about their experiences of working with clients from diverse backgrounds. A number of themes emerged that were relevant to countertransference. These include the therapists' observations that they needed to be able to tolerate anxiety, uncertainty, and also painful feelings such as racial guilt, when working with clients from minority groups. The participants commented on cultural differences in relation to race, gender, class, religion, and sexual identity and how these were reflected in transference and countertransference. Some reported a tendency to want to avoid talking about race/ethnic differences, although participants recognised that these cultural differences emerged in transference and countertransference reactions and were a central part of therapy (Tummala-Narra et al., 2018).

Minority group therapists

Comas-Diaz (2012) also observed that therapists from minority groups experience cultural countertransference. She observed a tendency for clients from the dominant culture to see the minority group professionals as belonging to a minority group first, and second, to see them as a professional. The cultural countertransference reactions for therapists from minority groups can include urges to engage in behaviours that prove their competence, feelings of anger or resentment for feeling they have to prove themselves, and attempting to avoid working with dominant culture clients (Comas-Diaz, 2012). Therapists can also be triggered by clients' culturally based transferences related to clients' defensiveness and lack of trust.

All of the participants in Tummala-Narra et al.'s (2018) study, who identified as belonging to an ethnic or sexual minority group, reported experiencing discrimination by clients, supervisors, and/or lecturers, and also reported that some clients made negative comments about their sociocultural group. Sometimes white clients did not continue with the minority therapist after the first session. Hence, therapists from a minority and mainstream background are likely to experience countertransference reactions that are evoked by cultural differences. Below are some brief vignettes that will allow you to explore how these issues may emerge in cross-cultural therapy.

Pause and reflect: Cases for discussion

A gay male client (Tom, Caucasian descent) experienced bullying as a teenager related to his sexual preference and is seeing a male therapist whom he perceives as heterosexual and a bit 'macho'. The male therapist feels that Tom is suspicious and untrusting of him, a feeling which he always struggles with. How might their relationship evolve?

A young British woman (Genia, Afro-Caribbean descent) is assigned to a woman therapist whom she perceives as 'upper crust'. The therapist listens as Genia reveals the poverty her family still experiences. This is very different from her wealthy upbringing. What issues might arise for both therapist and client?

A young Māori therapist (Kara) is working with a 15-year-old Māori girl (Ana) who is being bullied at school by Pākehā girls. The referring teacher who is Māori says that Ana's group of friends were also involved in the conflict with the Pākehā girls. She said, 'Both groups are responsible for what is happening'. Ana, however, seems to be more distressed about it than the other students and Kara can understand how she feels as she herself was bullied by Pākehā girls at school. What challenges does Ana face in working with Kara?

Viewing clients through a cultural lens

Finally, it is also important to note that psychological knowledge and theories, and psychotherapeutic practices used in Western countries have emerged mainly from European, British, and North American cultures. Psychotherapy training in Western countries has often reflected the cultural knowledge and practices of Western traditions and many aspects of these traditions do not fit with clients of different ethnic/racial backgrounds (Koç & Kafa, 2019). There is a risk that therapists will view clients and their struggles through their own culturally influenced psychotherapy theory and practice lens. While counselling, psychology, and psychotherapy professions emphasise the importance of cultural competence in their professional standards and ethics, there may be some way to go before many majority therapists are competent to work cross-culturally. This is one of the reasons given as an explanation for the findings that ethnic minority clients are much less likely to access and then maintain contact with mainstream therapy services (Knifton, 2012). As we discussed earlier, minority clients may not see themselves as validated or understood by practices based on Western psychotherapy. Viewing clients from the position of one's own cultural perspectives – values, beliefs systems, language, and cultural narratives – can be considered countertransferential as this involves viewing clients and their problems through a lens that does not fit, and therefore offering a psychotherapy service that does not meet the needs of the client.

Countertransference and professional and ethical behaviour

As therapists and trainees, we can find ourselves in complex situations with a number of competing factors to consider. Codes of ethical and professional conduct are important in situations where we are confronted with difficult situations that involve difficult decisions. We can think of codes of ethics or codes of conduct as important to follow in order to avoid engaging in behaviours that could lead to criticism or judgment from other professionals and clients. We can also view these codes as having a really positive role to fulfil in our lives as professionals – that is, to help keep us and our clients safe. When we are in doubt about how to behave in some situations, or feeling pulled in different directions in terms of our decision-making, we can reflect on the situation we are dealing with in the light of the guidelines provided by ethical standards.

Psychology, counselling, and psychotherapy ethics and conduct codes focus on a number of principles that aim to guide us in our decision-making in regard to our practices with clients. These are organised and presented somewhat differently across countries and professional bodies but share common concerns. These include the importance of making decisions that are in the best interest of the client, demonstrating respect for clients, acting in an honest and trustworthy way, working only with clients when competent to do so, and respecting diversity of clients and the equality, rights, and dignity of all people. Codes also emphasise the collective responsibilities of psychologists and psychotherapists for the welfare of people within the societies in which they live and work.

There is not much written about countertransference and ethical behaviour and there has been no research in this area as far as I am aware. The term countertransference is also not used in ethics codes. For example, the codes of the British Psychological Society (2018), American Psychological Society (2017), Australian Psychological Society (2007), New Zealand Psychological Society (2012) and the UK Council for Psychotherapy (2019) do not use the word countertransference. On the other hand, ethical codes of conduct are developed with the understanding that professionals in all walks of life are fallible and at risk of harm (as well as benefit) to clients in some situations. The codes recognise that we are subject to our own beliefs and biases, personal values, emotional reactions, and our own needs and desires – the latter of which can vary depending on our circumstances. As the BPS *Code of Ethics and Conduct* (2018) notes, our motivation and ability to engage in ethical reasoning and act on ethical standards can be compromised through competing biases:

> Maintaining awareness of such biases is important when trying to think through ethical challenges. These considerations currently include but are not limited to, salience (how readily something comes to mind), confirmation bias (the human tendency to look for evidence that confirms their belief and to ignore other evidence),

loss aversion (behaviour to avoid loss), beliefs about disclosure (tendency to be honest when they believe their actions will be known by others), and dissonance reduction (acting to maintain consistent beliefs). ... Psychologists are well placed and encouraged to consider these factors in their own decision-making. (p. 2)

Hence, from the understanding we have been developing about countertransference it becomes clear that countertransference reactions are likely, in some instances, to impact ethical reasoning or lead therapists to somehow avoid acknowledging that they are engaging, or thinking of engaging, in behaviours which are outside the safe boundaries of professional practice. I think too there is a general acceptance that countertransference reactions can influence therapists' decision-making and, in some situations, lead to problematic responses to clients that can have negative effects on clients and those around them.

In the section below, we will consider two scenarios in which countertransference reactions are leading therapists to consider engaging in what would be behaviours that could be deleterious for the client and for the therapeutic relationship. We will also reflect on sections of codes of practice that guide the therapist in appropriate behaviours given the circumstances.

Pause and reflect: Scenarios

Scenario one

Bob is a 32-year-old final year clinical psychology trainee. He has just broken up with his partner of 5 years and has to leave the apartment as it is in his partner's name. Bob is having difficulty finding another place to live as accommodation is really tight and also expensive in his university town. In the last session, one of Bob's older clients (a man in his seventies whose wife died six months previously) mentioned that an apartment he owned was becoming empty and he was looking for someone to take it over, someone he could rely on to look after it. Bob is thinking of asking his client if he could rent the apartment. He's been thinking that he could make sure that the client did not feel pressured but that it would be a solution for both of them. Bob thinks that his client would probably say Yes as his client seems to have a grandfatherly attitude towards Bob some of the time.

What are the ethical and professional issues relevant to Bob's decision?

Scenario two

Angela has been practising for three years. She places a lot of value on safe boundaries with clients. However, she is struggling currently. A client of hers is showing personal interest in her. The client compliments what she wears and how she looks. She shows interest in her thoughts and feelings. And last week she asked her if it would be possible to go out together once their therapy had ended. (They had another six sessions planned.) The client said she had never met anyone like Angela. Angela thought about it during the week and would really like to go out with her client. She is really attracted to her and feels this is different somehow in a positive way. She feels they were meant to be and she feels a bit relieved her supervisor is away as she really wants to think on this alone.

What are the ethical and professional issues relevant to Angela's decision?

Scenario one

In both the instances above, the therapists are at risk of putting their own needs – need for accommodation or a partner – before the needs of their clients. Bob is in a helping relationship with his client but is considering asking the client if he can rent his apartment. If he does this it is likely that the client's view of Bob as therapist will shift, and the client may begin to see Bob as someone who needs support rather than as someone who is there to support him. If Bob takes this action and the client accepts his proposal it will also lead to ongoing boundary issues as Bob will find himself in a position of regularly paying his client rent.

Bob is insecure currently because of the loss of his relationship with his partner and his home, and is at risk of convincing himself that renting his client's apartment would be mutually beneficial. This is an example of how our own needs can impact our thoughts and decision-making. Bob's reaction can be understood as a personal countertransference based on Bob's insecurity and needs at the current time. However, it is possible that there is an aspect of an objective countertransference in this situation. Bob's client, for example, is used to looking after others, and has a tendency to adopt a fatherly or paternal stance towards others. This paternal stance is, in part, a strategy that the client has developed as a way of coping with and minimising his own needs. Hence, Bob could be responding to a paternal attitude of the client towards him.

If Bob makes the suggestion and it is taken up by the client, it will be detrimental to their therapeutic relationship. Bob will have developed a dual relationship with his client – as his therapist and his tenant. Bob, as therapist, is the one who needs to take responsibility for protecting the therapeutic relationship from the difficulties associated with dual relationships. As the UK Council for Psychotherapy (2019) code states,

> Be aware of the power imbalance between the practitioner and client, and avoid dual or multiple relationships, which risk confusing an existing relationship and may impact adversely on a client. (p. 3)

Other aspects of codes are also relevant for Bob's decision-making. Codes of ethics generally emphasise the importance of prioritising the client's needs over self-interest. As an example, the British Psychological Society (2018) states that psychologists should act with integrity, which includes 'avoidance of exploitation and conflicts of interest (including self-interest)' and 'maintaining personal and professional boundaries' (p. 7). Hence, there is clear guidance available for Bob within the codes of practice. If Bob revisits his guidelines and reflects on these it will be clear to him that he should not consider asking to rent his client's apartment, nor take up an offer from the client should the client suggest it. This will preserve the relationship with safe and professional boundaries and enhance the likelihood that Bob will be helpful to his client.

On the other hand, it is important to note that Bob deserves some self-compassion. This is a difficult time. He is in training with all of the pressures that involves, and has lost his partner and his home. He will need support for this.

Scenario two

We will discuss sexual countertransference in Chapter 6. However, we can briefly discuss Angela's dilemma here. Angela has had personal experience of relationships that make her vulnerable in this situation. She has had difficulty finding a partner and she feels as if women generally are not very interested in her. She is aware that some of these feelings come from her relationships within her family but does not think this accounts for how she feels towards her client. The young woman client, on the other hand, has never had the type of attention that Angela is giving her now. The therapist seems so interested in her and so caring. She finds Angela's interest in her very sexy. Angela is also so different from her previous partner who was very self-centred. Rather Angela seems to really like hearing about her, she laughs at her jokes, and she seems to also really care. She really hopes that Angela will go out with her.

Angela feels attracted to her client and would like to take up her client's offer. She knows that this would be a 'bad thing' to do but it feels like the right thing to do. She revisits her ethics guidelines. These state that psychologists must not engage in sexual activity with a client, or within two years of the ending of the professional relationship, and even two years later, the psychologist must first explore, with a senior psychologist, if the client may be vulnerable and at risk of exploitation as a result of the previous professional relationship (Australian Psychological Society, 2007).

We discuss in Chapter 6 ways therapists can manage sexual attraction in therapy. What is important here is that Angela remembers that her role is to assist her client with the issues that she brought to therapy. However, it is also possible that Angela may struggle with her feelings of attraction to the client throughout the therapy. Angela's codes of ethics may help her to maintain the professional boundaries of the relationship but may not be enough to help her cope with her emotions in this situation. The activities that we learn about in Chapters 3 and 4 will assist Angela in this situation. She will be able to remind herself to centre herself and to remain in her therapist role with her client, while acknowledging that there is part of her that really wants to find a good partner. She can remind herself that it is just not possible with this person. It is also important that Angela talks this through with her supervisor when she returns and considers reflecting on it in her own therapy. Sharing this with her supervisor and her therapist is likely to be really helpful for Angela in remaining in a therapeutic position with her client and keeping herself and her client safe.

Pause and reflect: A case example

Here is another scenario for you to reflect on.

Jacqueline has 5 years' therapeutic experience and is just beginning to set up a part-time private practice. A transgender woman contacts Jacqueline and says that she would like some assistance with coping with 'coming out' at work. Jacqueline does not have any experience working with transgender women but would like to take on the client as the work could be interesting and it could help her build her practice. The woman tells Jacqueline on the phone that she has heard she is empathic and this is what she needs right now from a therapist. Jacqueline works hard at being empathic and values her empathic style. She thinks she could be good for this client.

What are the professional and/or ethical issues that arise here? And could Jacqueline's own personal issues influence her reaction to taking on the client, and if so, how?

Summary

This chapter considered the three components of the therapeutic relationship – the real relationship, the working alliance, and transference–countertransference – and their relationship to each other. In order to increase awareness of the nature of countertransference reactions, the chapter then examined different types of countertransference reactions reported by therapists and trainees, along with the types of reactions that experienced therapists/supervisors view as characteristic of countertransference. The chapter then differentiated between different aspects of countertransference – positive and negative countertransference, and subjective and objective countertransference.

The second part of the chapter turned to the question of cultural countertransference that arises in cross-cultural therapeutic relationships in which therapist and client are of different cultural backgrounds. It considered the types of transference and countertransference reactions that can be evoked in these situations. The chapter ended with a discussion of the relationship between countertransference and professional and ethical issues, and used therapy vignettes to illustrate the role that professional guidelines and codes of conduct can play in professional decision-making.

Recommended readings

Cartwright, C., Rhodes, P., King, R., & Shires, A. (2014). Experiences of countertransference: Reports of clinical psychology students. *Australian Psychologist, 49,* 232–240.

Comas-Diaz, L. (2012). *Multi-cultural care: A clinician's guide to cultural competence.* Washington, DC: American Psychological Association.

Comas-Diaz, L. & Jacobsen, F.M. (1991). Ethnocultural transference and countertransference in the therapeutic dyad. *American Journal of Orthopsychiatry, 61,* 392–402.

Hayes, J. A., Gelso, C. J., Goldberg, S., & Kivlighan, D. M. (2018). Countertransference management and effective psychotherapy: Meta-analytic findings. *Psychotherapy, 55,* 496–512.

Hofsess, C. D. & Tracey, T. J. (2010). Countertransference as a prototype: The development of a measure. *Journal of Counseling Psychology, 57,* 52–67.

Leahy, R. (2007). Schematic match in the therapeutic relationship: A social cognitive model. In P. Gilbert and R. Leahy (Eds.), *The therapeutic relationship in the cognitive behavioral psychotherapies* (pp. 229–254). New York, NY: Routledge.

3

Four Steps to Understanding and Managing Countertransference

This chapter introduces my four-step approach to understanding and managing countertransference. These four steps are: monitoring your responses to the client; reflecting on the client's patterns of relating to others; developing hypotheses about the interpersonal processes; and managing the countertransference reaction.

The four steps

1. Monitoring and being aware of countertransference responses.
2. Reflecting on the client's (and your) patterns of relating to others.
3. Developing hypotheses about the interpersonal processes.
4. Managing the countertransference reactions.

Before introducing these steps in more depth, we will consider the different psychotherapeutic concepts that are used in the four steps. These include self and other representations, which is a notion common to a number of therapies, and the Parent–Adult–Child (PAC) model first introduced by Eric Berne (1961, 1964) in his therapeutic approach, Transactional Analysis.

Self and other representations

Increasingly, there is a trend in psychology and psychotherapy towards viewing people as having multiple selves or self-states, in contrast to the notion of a unitary self (Safran & Muran, 2000). This view of multiple selves is complementary to a number of psychotherapeutic approaches and concepts, as will be discussed. In my approach, we use the concept of self–other representations to help us make sense of clients' experiences in therapy as well as our own. In order to understand transference and countertransference processes, it is helpful to reflect on clients' patterns of relating to others, as these patterns influence the ways in which they relate to us as therapists. In order to achieve this, we reflect on clients' life experiences and how these experiences have influenced the development of the clients' views of themselves (self-representations), views of others (other-representations) and views of relationships. It is also important for us to consider our own patterns of relating to others that we bring as therapists.

The concept of self and other representations (or self–other representations) is used in psychodynamic therapies such as object relations theory and attachment theory. Self–other representations can also be considered from CBT perspectives, using concepts of core beliefs or schema related to self, others, and relationships. These ideas are explored in more depth below, in relation to object relations theory, attachment theory, social-cognitive theory, and CBT.

Object relations theory

Object relations theory proposes that individuals develop internalised representations of relationships with significant others in everyday life. These internalisations of significant relationships are made up of units of self-and-object (other) representations (Kernberg, 2015; Stadter, 2016). These self–object representations are associated with affective states that can be positive or negative, contributing to an individual's personality style and underlying the types of relationships and relationship problems that the individual experiences. Negative self–object representations will be associated with negative feelings towards self and/or others, and will be accompanied by problematic interpretations or attributions of others' intentions and behaviours. In this way, an individual's negative experiences of significant relationships are acted out in current relationship problems that are characteristic of the client's presenting problems and ways of relating to the therapist.

Attachment theory

Bowlby (1973) was initially influenced by object relations theory and was interested in understanding how internalised object relations developed in infants.

He proposed that infants – through repeated interactions with their caregivers – form mental representations of self and other/s. Bowlby believed that these representations or inner working models consisted of expectations, beliefs, and/or rules for behaving and thinking that an infant/child uses within relationships (Fraley & Shaver, 2008). Once developed, these representations of self and other/s, along with the inner working model of relationships, influence individuals' emotional and behavioural reactions to events within relationships. A child with a secure attachment to caregivers is likely to have both positive representations of others (as caring, reliable, safe) and positive representations of self (as lovable, safe, trusting). A child with an insecure attachment, on the other hand, is developing some negative representations of others (such as distant, unavailable, unreliable) and of self (such as unlovable, alone, needy). Research suggests that these inner working models not only influence how a person relates to others but also the kinds of reactions that are elicited from others (Fraley & Shaver, 2008). These inner working models of relationships and the associated self–other representations thereby provide templates for relationships, and in therapy will shape clients' transference reactions and also influence therapists' countertransference reactions.

A social-cognitive model

Andersen and colleagues (Andersen & Berk, 1998; Miranda & Andersen, 2007) have investigated transference in non-therapeutic contexts using a social-cognitive model of transference. According to Andersen's model, representations of significant others exist in memory and these representations can be activated in social interactions by cues that are relevant to a representation of the other (such as a tone of voice, similar features, a style of interacting), leading to a transference reaction. When an other-representation, and thereby transference, is activated, the person experiencing the transference sees the other person through the lens of a pre-existing representation/s. An important aspect of this is that representations of self and other are paired, and when the transference is triggered by relevant cues in the environment, then so too is the other side of the coin – the representation of self. On the other hand, when a representation of self is triggered, so too is the paired representation of other.

Pause and reflect: Mani's self–other representations

Mani is really enjoying talking to a friend, Amie, about their Christmas holidays. Amie is interrupted by someone she knows and the two hug and start to chat animatedly. Mani feels deflated. As it continues, he feels hurt and angry. Amie's friend says good-bye after about three minutes and Amie turns back to resume her chat with Mani. By this time, Mani has gone off Amie and really doesn't

(Continued)

want to talk anymore. He makes an excuse and leaves. He thinks about Amie as being mean and rejecting and he feels a bit awful about himself too, as if he is not interesting enough for Amie, compared to her other friend.

Mani is not aware of it but he may have experienced the activation of a self–other representation. If this (feeling rejected by others) is a fairly common type of experience for Mani, what might be a self and other representation/s that he has developed through his life experiences? Think of these in terms of pairs, for example:

Self as ..../Other as......................................

We can also think about Mani's reactions from an attachment perspective. If feeling rejected by others and then turning away from them (and feeling critical towards himself and them) is a common experience for Mani, we can hypothesise that Mani has an insecure attachment style. It is possible that Mani experienced rejection or a lack of consistency in his relationships with caregivers that now results in a sensitivity to feeling rejected and having angry thoughts and feelings towards the perceived rejecting person and also towards himself.

Of course, we cannot know and assume this, but it is helpful for the psychotherapeutic process to observe themes in clients' ways of relating to others and then to consider the origins of these relationship themes. The validity of any hypotheses you develop can then be assessed through further exploration of clients' formative experiences.

In a social-cognitive model, as with the previous theories, these representations of self and other are viewed as leading to interpersonal patterns of relating that are placed onto new individuals (Andersen & Berk, 1998). While transference is a normal process – something we all engage in throughout everyday life – placing old patterns, especially troubled ones or even idealising ones, onto new relationships perpetuates problematic interactional processes for the individual involved. Mani, for example, lost the opportunity to continue to enjoy his chat with Amie and to further build their friendship. Instead, he pushed Amie away and was left feeling bad – both towards himself and Amie. This is likely to have impacted on Amie and she might be more cautious about talking to Mani again. This in turn will reinforce Mani's self–other representations.

Hence, the concept of self–other representations is compatible with a number of therapeutic approaches and is useful for understanding our own and our clients' templates for relationships that they and we bring to therapy.

Below is another vignette for you to consider. Ana begins therapy with an idealised representation of other. I will discuss my way of understanding this but first you can use the concept of self–other representations to reflect on what is happening for Ana.

CASE STUDY: ANA'S STORY

Ana's mother was sick a lot when she was a child. She got lots of care from others around her, including her father, her aunties, and her grandparents. On the other hand, she had to give lots of care to her two younger siblings. For as long as she can remember, Ana has had a feeling of yearning for someone she could really rely on – someone who would care for her and take away the sense of hollowness she feels inside. She day-dreamed throughout her childhood about having a wonderful woman who cared for her and looked after her.

Ana was struggling at the age of 28 years with feelings of emptiness and depression. A friend of Ana's recommended a woman therapist whom she described as wonderful and really caring. Ana had her first session with the therapist and felt elated afterwards. She really, really liked her. She felt so at home with her and, yes, the therapist was very caring, as she had been described. Ana was so looking forward to seeing her again and felt elated about her next appointment. On the morning of the appointment, however, the receptionist rang to say that the therapist was unwell and could not make her appointment this week. She re-organised the appointment for the following week.

Ana went from feeling elated at being able to see her therapist again, to feeling as if she were crashing into an empty hole. She began to cry and it was difficult to pull herself together to get to work. During the day, she tried to tell herself she was being ridiculous – the therapist was sick, she would be back at work soon, it would be OK. But the positive feelings about having found this therapist were gone. She was up and down for the week and became nervous before her next session with the therapist. She thought of cancelling but her good sense told her not to.

In order to practise using the concept of self–other representations, you can complete the brief exercise below and then compare your ideas to the ones I discuss below.

Pause and reflect: Ana's story

Having reflected on Ana's experiences as a child and then her reactions to the therapist's cancelling, what paired self–other representation/s do you think Ana may have developed through her childhood experiences?

Self as ..../Other as....................................

Self as ..../Other as....................................

I hypothesise that Ana experienced a lack of consistent caring during her childhood, despite her family's best efforts. She appears to carry a sense of loss and/or emptiness in her everyday life, although this may come and go depending on what is happening in her life. While we do not know enough about Ana to be confident about self–other representations, it seems possible that she has representations of self as alone and vulnerable, perhaps as abandoned or unwanted, and also as unable to cope. She may have representations of others as unavailable, uncaring, or unreliable.

Given her recollections of day-dreaming about an all-caring other, and how she reacted to meeting the therapist and her response to the cancellation, she may also have developed an idealised other-representation during her childhood years in which she yearned for and fantasised about having a caring woman to look after and comfort her, to help her feel better and take away the sense of emptiness. The self-representation that goes with this idealised other-representation is likely to be seeing herself as safe, cared for, and perhaps special. Ana is unlikely to be conscious of or understand this, although this understanding may emerge in therapy. Instead, at this time in her life, Ana may still have a yearning to have someone – perhaps someone special – to help her feel better.

The cancellation of her session has triggered a shift in self–other representations. The self-representation/s and the associated emotions she is now experiencing are negative and are associated with her experiences of having been unsupported during her mother's illnesses and absences. She is approaching her next session with anxiety. She has lost the sense of elation she experienced in relation to her idealised other and is feeling really down and vulnerable. There will be an opportunity for the therapist to explore this with Ana if she notices a change in Ana's attitude towards her. We will discuss relevant strategies that the therapist could use in the next chapter. But what is important to understand here is that, sometimes, idealised representations are developed through the absence of a desired other/s in the life of the child and these can act as a defence against unbearable feelings – that is, fantasising or imagining having an idealised other can help a child manage emotions that threaten to overwhelm.

Cognitive-behavioural therapy perspectives

As mentioned above, the psychodynamic concept of self and other representations can be understood within CBT perspectives. CBT therapists use concepts such as core beliefs or schemas in their cognitive formulations and cognitive interventions. While CBT therapists appear to focus more on core beliefs about self, they can also consider core beliefs held about others. Reflecting on core beliefs about others that are linked to beliefs about self is likely to be a helpful part of a CBT formulation – for example, the belief that the self is inadequate and helpless may be linked to beliefs about others as judgmental or, alternatively, as superior. The emotions attached to these beliefs may be hurt, anger, or feelings of worthlessness and/or vulnerability.

Using CBT concepts to think about Ana, I would propose that Ana has a problematic core belief of self that developed as a result of her mother's illnesses and absences. She also had to learn to be unselfish and care for her siblings, perhaps in order to maintain adult approval. She may have a core belief of self as abandoned and unwanted, and core beliefs of others as abandoning on the one hand, or as strong on the other. These beliefs are associated with feelings of vulnerability – feeling alone and unable to cope, and with a sense of loss and yearning.

The Parent–Adult–Child model

As you will see later in the chapter, the third step focuses on developing hypotheses about the interpersonal processes that are occurring in the therapeutic relationship. As noted earlier, there has been a trend towards psychotherapeutic approaches rejecting the notion of a unitary self as opposed to considering the multiple aspects of the self or self-states that are experienced by individuals and that compete for dominance (Safran & Muran, 2000). The majority of us, for example, will experience times when we are calm, comfortable, and confident, and other times when we feel anxious, self-doubting, and self-critical. Therapists also experience these different subjectivities themselves in their work with clients.

In the four-step approach, I use the model of Parent–Adult–Child (PAC) (see Figure 3.1), as this provides a visual map for thinking about potential transference and countertransference reactions. The PAC model has been used previously by other therapists to reflect on transference and countertransference (e.g., Bateman, Brown & Pedder, 2000; Clarkson, 1992).

The PAC model is accessible and is adapted and used by therapists from different approaches. It originated in the psychodynamic approach Transactional Analysis (TA), developed by Eric Berne (1961, 1964). In line with other psychotherapeutic approaches, Berne observed that individuals shift between different ways of experiencing themselves and others. He called these ego-states. The term ego-state refers to our subjective reactions – our feelings, thoughts, urges, behaviours (about and towards ourselves, others, and situations in our lives) – that we experience at any point in time. He thought that we experience three main states, which he titled Parent, Adult, and Child.

When a person is in an Adult ego-state, they are responding to the present situation in a realistic way in the here and now, using the personal resources they have.

When they shift into a Parent ego-state, they shift into a way of thinking, feeling, and behaving which is parental towards the other/s and/or themselves in the situation. They may have learnt these ways of responding from adult caregivers and authority figures in childhood. When they shift into a Child ego-state, they are reacting to the current situation in ways similar to how they reacted in childhood. See Figure 3.1 for an illustration of the PAC model.

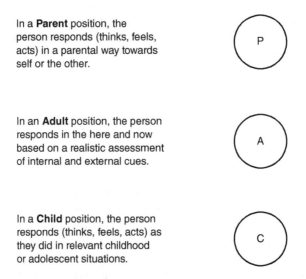

In a **Parent** position, the person responds (thinks, feels, acts) in a parental way towards self or the other.

In an **Adult** position, the person responds in the here and now based on a realistic assessment of internal and external cues.

In a **Child** position, the person responds (thinks, feels, acts) as they did in relevant childhood or adolescent situations.

Figure 3.1   The Parent–Adult–Child (PAC) model

As therapists, we are likely to be most comfortable and at our therapeutic best when we are in an Adult ego-state or Adult self. As therapists, we aim to empathically attune to our clients and to respond at any given moment in a way that is helpful for the client. This assists us to stay in our Adult self. However, just as our clients are triggered into Child or Parental states, so can we be. One simple way of reflecting on whether our reactions are counter-transferential is to ask ourselves if we have been triggered and shifted out of our Adult self into a Child or Parent state.

Being in the Parent or the Child

How does a client behave when they are in a Child state?

Clients can become playful or distracting, they can share their joy with you, they can feel hurt or threatened and withdraw, they can get in touch with sadness or grief and cry, they can get angry and withdraw into a hurt, vulnerable position, and they can become distant or dissociated.

How does a client behave when they shift into a Parent state?

Clients can be protective of therapists (and themselves), they can act in caring or concerned ways towards you as their therapist, they can praise you, they can criticise or tell you off, they can act in superior ways towards you, and they can use strategies to exert control over you.

Ego-states and schema modes

It might be helpful for some readers who are interested in Schema Therapy to compare concepts of ego-states and schema modes. This may also be helpful for some readers as it can be useful to see the links or similarities in different psycho-therapeutic approaches. Schema modes, similar to ego-states, refer to the emotional states and coping responses we experience and use in everyday life (Young, Klosko, & Weishaar, 2003). Schema modes are triggered in everyday life situations to which we are sensitive, and can be both adaptive and maladaptive. While TA proposes three ego-states (Parent, Adult, and Child), Young and colleagues in their Schema Therapy propose four main types of mode. These include child modes, maladaptive coping modes, dysfunctional parent modes, and the healthy adult mode. They also propose four child modes – the vulnerable child, angry child, impulsive/undisciplined child, and the happy child.

Pause and reflect: Mani and the PAC model

Thinking about using the PAC model, we could think about Mani as having been in his Adult – calm and behaving in a friendly way towards Amie. He then shifted when she began talking to her friend. He may have shifted to a hurt Child position and/or he may also have shifted to a critical Parent position – towards himself ('No-one likes me. There is something wrong with me') and towards Amie ('She is mean. She is not worth my time'). Alternatively, he may have initially gone into a hurt Child and then shifted into an angry Parent state, in part to protect himself from the hurt. We could think of this as a coping strategy or a defensive process, in which Mani defends himself from his hurt Child feelings, which may be associated with quite painful childhood emotions and memories.

Can you think of a time recently when you were triggered out of your Adult self into either a Child or Parent self? What happened for you?

Ana's experience

We can also reflect on Ana's experience using the PAC model. I hypothesise that Ana was in a happy, elated Child state looking forward to her next session with her idealised other/parent/therapist. When her session was cancelled, Ana shifted into a different Child state – one in which she felt as if she were 'crashing into an empty hole'. As her next session approached, she also began to feel anxious and to think about cancelling – perhaps moving into a hurt, vulnerable Child state and wanting to withdraw from the therapist.

Self–other representations and the PAC model

The notion of self–other representations uses language different from the PAC model, so how can we understand the relationship between Parent, Adult, or Child states and self–other representations? In my approach, the PAC states refer to the subjective reactions and responses that the person experiences when a self–other representation is triggered. Self-representations are developed mainly through formative experiences, so the self-representation links most strongly to the Child in the PAC model. The other-representation links strongly to the Parent and this can be either a nurturing or caring Parent state or a critical or controlling Parent state.

Countertransference responses can therefore be viewed as involving a shift out of the Adult – the therapist shifts into a Child-state or a Parent-state. The Adult also represents a position to which therapists can shift when they notice that they have moved into a Parent-state or Child-state in relation to the client. Importantly, the therapeutic alliance can be represented by the Adult-to-Adult position (Brown & Pedder, 1991). See Figure 3.2 for a representation of the therapeutic alliance using the PAC model.

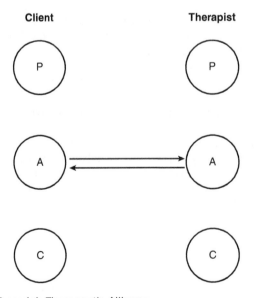

Figure 3.2 The PAC model: Therapeutic Alliance

The four steps

Having considered the concepts used in this approach, we will now discuss the four steps that make up this approach to understanding and managing our countertransference reactions.

Step One: Monitoring and being aware of countertransference responses

The first step in being able to understand and manage countertransference reactions is to be aware of them. Two early studies of countertransference found that awareness of countertransference and having a theoretical perspective for understanding it were associated with fewer countertransference behaviours; on the other hand, having a theoretical perspective of countertransference but *not* being aware of one's own countertransference reactions was associated with *higher* rates of countertransference behaviours (Latts & Gelso, 1995; Robbins & Jolkovski, 1987). Hence, awareness of our own responses is essential.

Sometimes, though, countertransference is hard to recognise. We can think, for example, that we are having a 'normal' reaction to something the client has said or done and not question why we are having that particular reaction, or we might not name it as countertransference as it feels like something to do with us and not related to our client. As one trainee who completed training in this four-step approach said:

> My awareness of countertransference responses has increased substantially since doing this course. I am much more aware of my countertransference reactions and less likely to attribute everything I am experiencing to my own inadequacies or feelings of incompetence.

Hence, the initial step involves learning to monitor our emotional reactions in therapy situations. As discussed previously, countertransference emotions take many forms, including feeling warm and loving or protective towards clients, experiencing anger, hurt, embarrassment, humiliation, frustration, stuckness, and so on.

While our emotional reactions tend to be most salient in sessions, our countertransference reactions also include bodily/physiological, cognitive, and behavioural components. We tend to emphasise our emotions when we talk about countertransference, as the emotional aspect may be at the forefront of our attention and have greater valence for us. Yet, it is also important to tune into your cognitions or thoughts. We might not be consciously aware of these at the time – in a similar way that we are often not aware of what CBT therapists call our automatic thoughts. Our thoughts might be about the client ('She's really intelligent ... much more than me', 'She's so sophisticated', 'He's deliberately blocking me', 'He doesn't really want to get better', 'He's so gorgeous!', 'This client does not like me', 'They think I don't understand'), or our thoughts might be about the therapy ('This is going nowhere', 'This is going great', 'I can't bear to hear about this') and yourself as therapist ('I'm hopeless at this', 'I can't manage this client', 'I think I am really suited to this type of work', 'I'm really dumb', 'I need to read a lot more about this'). Trainees and beginning therapists are also likely to have thoughts around how well they are doing and how they will be evaluated by the supervisor or other observers ('What will my supervisor think? I can't tell my supervisor how I feel towards this client, she will think I am unsafe!').

Further, as a CBT approach points out, imagery can also be thought of as a form of cognition. While CBT tends to emphasise client cognition and its relationship to psychopathology, some and perhaps many therapists also experience imagery when working with clients. In a study I conducted with colleagues, therapists were asked to write about recent experiences of imagery (Cartwright, Cowie, Bavin, & Bennett-Levy, 2019). Some of the examples that were provided of therapist imagery appeared to reflect experiences within the therapeutic relationship and in some instances countertransference – for example, one therapist recalled an image of their hands around a client's neck in the context of a tense relationship, and another recalled knocking at a door with nobody answering when working with an uncommunicative client. These images are evocative and useful in that they alert the therapist to possible countertransference. They may also provide some understanding of the nature of our reactions and be informative about what the client might be experiencing.

It is also important to notice any bodily or physiological reactions. These will also help you to understand your countertransference reaction and its meaning for you. These could include many types of bodily reactions, such as feeling tense, tightness in the chest, an ache around the heart, becoming breathless, feeling hot all over, having clenched fists, or becoming sleepy. With this latter, you might think you feel a bit sleepy with a client because you usually see them after lunch when you have an energy slump. However, you might also find that you have this same experience if the client comes in first thing in the morning.

Finally, it is also important to monitor any urges towards actions that we experience in therapy, along with our behaviours and ways of relating to clients. It is quite common to experience urges in therapy, for example, to feel like you want to take clients home and look after them, phone up their partners and tell them off, end sessions with them, or argue with them. Sometimes we give into these urges or we make decisions about how to respond based on our countertransference and engage in countertransference behaviours. We might not recognise these as such until later. For example, trainees in our study (discussed in Chapter 2) reported working hard to 'fix' a client, doing an incomplete assessment as a result of minimising the client's difficulties, prematurely ending sessions with a client, finishing sentences for a client, struggling to find the right words when talking to the client, and having difficulty behaving in an empathic way with a client (Cartwright et al., 2014).

The aim of this book is to help therapists be aware of their countertransference reactions, and have ways of understanding these reactions and using them, if appropriate. Hence, the first step involves a commitment to monitoring your emotional, cognitive, physiological/bodily, and behavioural responses to clients and the therapy situation. This might sound like a lot to be aware of, especially for those who are in an early stage of working therapeutically. Initially, it can be difficult to tune into the client, tune into yourself, continue to assess and formulate the client's problems, and think about how you are going to respond to what they just did or said in therapy, given your therapy plan. However, as you practise this more, you will find it easier – not that countertransference is ever very easy!

Almost all of the trainees and therapists who completed a one- or two-day training in this four-step approach reported some time after the training that they had increased their awareness of their countertransference reactions. Some written comments included:

> I am more aware of my own countertransference responses. I find myself questioning myself a bit more over the more subtle countertransference reactions I have.

> I have become more consciously aware of countertransference occurring in session. I now notice countertransference more frequently when working with clients and also in my interactions with others.

Initially, it might work better to simply notice how you are responding in sessions and reflect on it after sessions. Schön (1987) referred to the process of reflecting at the time as reflecting in action. Reflecting after the session can be thought of as reflecting on action. You can also reflect on action in supervision. As another trainee said:

> I now notice countertransference more often. In session, I mainly notice my reactions to clients, then I take this to supervision to formulate what might be contributing to my reactions and to discuss how to manage it in the next session, so that it is therapeutic for the client.

Reflecting *in* and *on* action are both important aspects of reflective practice and are essential in terms of developing the abilities to understand and manage countertransference. In Step Four, we will look more closely at strategies that you can use in the moment to manage your countertransference so that you can minimise the frequency of countertransference behaviours.

> ## Pause and reflect: Observing countertransference reactions
>
> Take a moment to think about a recent countertransference reaction you have had. What was happening between you and the client and how were you feeling? What thoughts or ideas or images were going through your mind? What bodily reactions were you having, if any? What did you feel like doing or saying? And, what did you actually do?
>
> In the next week or two, it might also be helpful to begin to consciously monitor your countertransference reactions and to reflect on how aware you are of your countertransference. You could also focus on attuning to the different elements of your reactions including your emotions, your thoughts/imagery, bodily reactions, urges, and behaviours. Then, you could observe how your awareness changes over time, as you read this book, and apply the ideas to your practice. If you feel it is helpful, you could keep a reflective diary and discuss some of your reactions with your supervisor/s.

Step Two: Reflecting on the client's patterns of relating to others

During this step, we reflect on clients' patterns of relating by using the concept of self–other representations. To be able to do this, we need to begin to understand clients' developmental histories, the types of relationships they had with primary caregivers, and other formative experiences that may have shaped their beliefs about self, other, and relationships. This will include experiences that they have had because of their sociocultural backgrounds. Later, we will also think about the themes that are present in relationships in their current everyday lives, as they talk about them, and finally, as therapy progresses, we reflect on how clients are relating to us in therapy and how we are responding to them.

In order to demonstrate this process, I will use vignettes from the therapy sessions of a client we shall call Mary and her therapist Patrick.

INTRODUCTION TO MARY

Mary was 39 years old. She was single but had always wanted to have a partner and children. However, she had a history of short-lived relationships and was starting to feel quite desperate about where she was in life. This is why she began therapy with Patrick.

Mary recalled that her parents spent a lot of time together and seemed very close, although they were not very demonstrative with each other. She described her parents as a 'tight-knit unit'. They made her go to bed early, from as long as she can remember, so that they could have 'together time'. They left her with carers a lot. They also went away on holidays together and left her with her grandparents. At the dinner table, they talked mainly between themselves. Mary says she did get some attention. One of them read her a story at night. They made her breakfast, lunch, and dinner. They took her out to a park or played a game together as a family on the weekend. But generally she remembers feeling like it was hard to get attention and often felt quite pushed away and rejected by both of them when they ignored her. She recalled feeling quite desperate to get their attention and at times was 'beside herself'. When she was younger, she threw tantrums. She recalled wrapping herself around her mother's legs and crying. She remembered doing this when she was around four years old when her parents were going off to work together and leaving her with a carer. When she did this, though, her parents became really irritated with her, said she was being naughty, and held her away. She also recalled deliberately spilling her food during dinner at around that time and bursting into tears at the dinner table a few times when she was around six to eight, in order, she thinks now, to get attention. When she did this, her parents just got angry with her, and put her in her bedroom or told her off. Mary says that, over time, she continued to feel left out, and hurt and angry, but she tried not to feel like this and to behave well, in order to get her parents' approval. She continued though to have angry, hurt outbursts with her parents occasionally during her teenage years, although she never talked to them about how she felt. Whenever she showed any distress, they became 'cool' with her, withdrawing further from her until she went back to acting as if nothing was wrong.

MARY'S SELF–OTHER REPRESENTATIONS

There appears to be a theme of feeling shut out, left alone, and/or pushed away in Mary's stories of her relationship with her parents. The 'other' in the stories of parents is experienced as rejecting, dismissing, and/or uncaring. The self, on the other hand, is left out, rejected, and at times desperate in her sense of loneliness.

Initially, then, I might reflect that a key self–other representation held by Mary is *self as rejected/hurt* and *other/s as rejecting/dismissive/uncaring*. The emotions associated with these representations appear to include feeling hurt and angry and, at times, desperate. Mary may also have experienced anxiety and fear as she felt left alone a lot by her parents. When Mary expressed any of her emotions, however, she felt disapproved of by her parents - feeling further pushed aside or rebuked.

As we get to know clients better, we might refine the words that we use to try to capture the self–other representations that link to Mary's experiences and also the emotions that go with these. You might also use different wording to that I have used. When I engage in this activity, I try to find words that best capture the essence of the client's experiences of self in relation to other/s, as the client portrays them in sessions.

Pause and reflect: Your self–other representations

Do your hypothesised self–other representations for Mary differ from what I have proposed so far?

If so, what self–other representations might fit for Mary and her experience of herself in relation to others?

Self as ..../ and Other as ....

Self as ..../ and Other as ....

MARY'S POSITIVE SELF–OTHER REPRESENTATIONS

The representations considered above are negative, in the sense that they are associated with negative thoughts and feelings about self, others, and relationships, and are likely to be problematic for Mary when they are triggered in everyday life. However, Mary will have had other relationships and experiences. Below is further information about Mary's relationships that may have impacted on the development of self–other representations.

Mary did quite well academically at school and had one or two friends during most years of her schooling. She didn't like hanging out with bigger groups because she tended to feel insignificant, especially with 'popular' girls. Mary also liked spending time with her favourite teachers whenever she could, although they seemed to get irritated with her if she hung around them too much. When she was at high school, she also talked to school counsellors when she got the opportunity. She did not talk about anything very important but they made her feel cared about. At home she continued to feel lonely a lot of the time, although there were good times too, when she spent some individual time with one of her parents, or they did something together and included her. She loved this. She also loved her grandparents as she was their only granddaughter and they really seemed to care about her and want her company.

Hence, Mary is also likely to hold some positive self–other representation/s. She has had caring grandparents, some friends at school, and some support from teachers and school counsellors. She also had some good times with her parents. She may have a *representation of self as cared for* and *others as caring*. This representation may be activated more in situations in which she feels she belongs or is accepted. However, Mary is likely to shift into a negative representation when there are triggers in relationships.

In order to understand Mary's self–other representations, we have reflected on the themes in her relationships with her parents and others in her life. With clients, generally it is helpful to focus on their history of relationships from our first contact with them and pay attention to the ways in which they talk about themselves in relation to others – from when they were children through to current times. We can then reflect on the self–other representations underlying these relationship themes.

In the next section, we will reflect on Patrick, the therapist, and a self–other representation/s he holds that will make working with Mary challenging for him.

Patrick felt a lot of compassion for Mary during the first four sessions as they talked through her history and he imagined what it would be like to feel as an outsider to her parents' relationship with each other. He thought she had done well in her life given this and that she was quite resourceful growing up.

Patrick's story was different. Patrick's parents got on quite well but his father was away a lot with his work, and when this happened, his mother would become more emotional and more 'clingy' with him, as the oldest child of three. He remembers times at around the age of nine or ten when he would be sitting on the couch and his mother would sit beside him, put her arms around his shoulders and tell him everything would be OK, that they would do OK with his father away. This really annoyed Patrick as he had been feeling fine and felt that his mother was feeling bad but not really saying so and putting it onto him. He used to feel like pushing her away from him, although he didn't because he also thought that would make it worse for her and then for himself. He was relieved at age 13 when his father changed his job and no longer went away as part of his work. His mother seemed to become more secure.

Patrick had also noticed in his own life that he did not 'handle clingy women very well' and had chosen a partner who was strong and independent. Patrick had also noticed a tendency in himself to want to withdraw when women clients seemed 'needy' and had consciously attempted to address this.

PATRICK'S SELF AND OTHER REPRESENTATIONS

We don't know as much about Patrick as we do Mary. However, we know that he perceived that he struggled with 'clingy' women and that he had a strong emotional response to what he experienced as his mother's clinginess. To think about this some more, we can put ourselves in Patrick's place. What would it have been like to be a 10-year-old boy whose mother was anxious and insecure when your father was away and she turned to you for comfort and support?

This could feel like quite a lonely position to be in and could also feel frightening and unsafe, not having an adult who is creating a safe place, although it's important to note that Patrick at that age may not have been aware of these feelings. Patrick also disliked the way his mother acted as if she was comforting him but was using him to comfort herself. He wanted to push her away. We could hypothesise that Patrick has a *representation of self as vulnerable/ overwhelmed* and *other as needy/demanding*. The emotions associated with these representations may include feeling frightened/insecure, angry/rejecting, and perhaps guilty.

Pause and reflect: Patrick's self–other representations

Do you agree with my tentative ideas about possible self–other representations? What alternatives might you propose?

Self as ..../Other as.....................................
Self as ..../Other as.....................................

Step Three: Developing hypotheses about the interpersonal processes

This step combines our understanding of the client's patterns of relating to others (self–other representations) with the PAC model in order to reflect on the interpersonal processes that occur between therapist and client. The aim of this step is to develop valid hypotheses about what is happening between the client and therapist in the session in order to understand or conceptualise the therapist's countertransference reaction. In order to illustrate this, we will reflect on some events in the fifth and sixth sessions of therapy with Patrick and Mary.

THERAPY EVENTS IN THE FIFTH AND SIXTH THERAPY SESSIONS

In the fifth session, Mary and Patrick talked in more depth about what Mary referred to as her 'failed relationships'. She said that they began well, went well for a while, and then began to deteriorate. She said that she had chosen the wrong men – men who were selfish and not willing to meet her needs. She talked about how they always started to push her away after a few months together and how devastating this was for her. During this session, Patrick began to feel irritated with Mary as Mary talked 'on and on' about how much she had been let down in life, especially by male partners. Patrick also found it difficult to end the session on time. Mary seemed to want to keep talking and getting off her chest just how badly she had been treated. Patrick did his best to empathise but continued to feel some irritation at times. He hoped it did not show on his face.

In the sixth session, Patrick knew that he needed to remind Mary that he was taking two weeks leave in four weeks' time. Patrick had told Mary about his annual leave before they began therapy and she said it would not be a problem. However, Patrick understood that therapist absences can be disruptive for clients and people leaving her (parents and partners) had been painful for Mary in the past. Prior to the session, Patrick felt some anxiety about telling Mary and thought through how he would remind her. He decided to do it gently and at the beginning of the session when he reflected back on what they had been talking about and where they were going in sessions. When he did remind Mary about his upcoming absence at the beginning of the sixth session, she began to talk about her feelings of loneliness and her desperation to have a family. She said that she did not think she could be happy if she had to go through life without a child and her own family. She began comparing herself to her friends who had their own children and how lucky they were. She started crying as she talked about her age and how she didn't have time to waste.

As Mary continued to talk like this, Patrick had an urge to get up and go out of the room. He then realised he had a sense that Mary was clinging to him and he wanted to push her off or push her away, or to somehow get away from her. He also experienced an image of her as a child clinging onto her mother's knees and her mother trying to push her away to leave. Patrick tried to stay centred and be empathic towards Mary. In reflecting on his reaction after the session, Patrick realised that his feeling of being clung to by his mother had been triggered in the session.

TRANSFERENCE AND COUNTERTRANSFERENCE IN THE FIFTH AND SIXTH SESSIONS

In the fifth session, Mary and Patrick talked through her history of relationships with partners. This appeared to evoke feelings of distress and anger in Mary as she talked about the men who had rejected her. In turn, Patrick shifted from previously feeling mainly empathic towards Mary to feeling irritated with her at times. He had negative thoughts about how blaming she was to others and how she must have contributed to the problems. When he felt irritated with her, he wondered if he was moving into a critical Parent and if she was transferring a negative parental figure on to him.

Then in the sixth session, Patrick reminded Mary of the break in upcoming sessions. She responded to this with expressions of distress and some desperation about her life. Patrick felt irritated with Mary, as in the previous session. However, his countertransference was stronger this session. He had a strong sense of Mary clinging to him. He felt a strong urge to leave the session or to pull away from her or push her away.

We can use the PAC model to consider what happened between Mary and Patrick as Patrick experienced this countertransference. Mary's outward behaviour and words suggest that she moved into a vulnerable Child state (self-representation) in which she felt desperate about her life situation and being alone for the rest of her life. This appears to have been triggered by Patrick reminding her of the future break in sessions. In his countertransference, Patrick experienced Mary as needy and had a strong sense of her clinging to him. He had an urge to push her away or off him or to get out of the room. He appears to have shifted into a critical Parent (other-representation), wanting to get away from her clinging to him.

We can understand this as a *complementary countertransference* in which Patrick identified with Mary's transference to him as a critical or abandoning other. See Figure 3.3 for a representation of this complementary countertransference.

CLIENT – MARY   **THERAPIST – PATRICK**

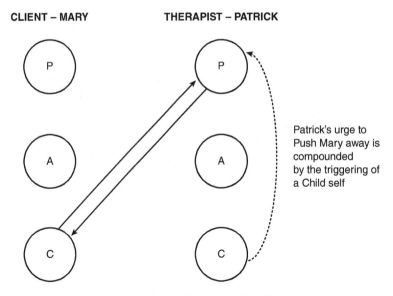

Patrick's urge to Push Mary away is compounded by the triggering of a Child self

Figure 3.3   A complementary countertransference with subjective elements

If this hypothesis is valid, then Mary and Patrick are repeating a relationship theme that has been central for Mary throughout her life. Mary feared and expected abandonment. Patrick responded to her distressed reactions in a complementary way, taking up the role of the rejecting/abandoning parent/ other in his need to push her away and be rid of her clinginess.

A COMPLEMENTARY COUNTERTRANSFERENCE WITH SUBJECTIVE ELEMENTS

As noted above, Mary and Patrick have re-created an important emotional theme that is central to Mary's life – one in which she expects abandonment and rejection and the other responds in an abandoning or rejecting way. However, Mary's reaction to Patrick going away has also triggered an emotional reaction that Patrick still feels in regard to his mother's clinginess with him as a child. We can understand this as Patrick also having a subjective countertransference reaction to Mary's clinginess, which has added to Patrick's challenge, as it compounds the complementary countertransference. I have represented this with the dotted line from Patrick's Child to his Parent in Figure 3.3.

Pause and reflect: Complementary countertransference

This type of countertransference, in which the therapist identifies with or takes up the role or representation of other is called a complementary countertransference. In this type of countertransference, we therapists become the other – the neglecting hurtful other, the abandoning other, the incompetent other, the idealised other, the rescuing other, or the one who will be different to all the others.

Can you think of a recent time when you have had a complementary countertransference to a client? How did this emerge?

A RELATIONAL PERSPECTIVE

You will remember that we talked in Chapter 1 about a relational perspective of countertransference. If we think of this interaction from that perspective, we can see that Patrick has become embedded in Mary's pattern of relating to others, in which she struggles to hold on to others and they push her away or reject her. He may be particularly susceptible to this because of his personal history and sensitivities. However, it is not a bad thing that this has happened. It is part of therapy and the therapeutic relationship, and by becoming part of a client's relational patterns, we may come to understand the client – and how others experience them – in a deeper and more intuitive way. It is about being in a relationship with the client and it is about learning about their inner world. As Heimann (1950) said, our countertransference is a mirror reflection of the client's inner world. Patrick's challenge is to shift out of this embeddedness and to find a way of responding to Mary that will be helpful to her.

Pause and reflect: The three questions

To assist us in our reflections, we can use the three questions that were discussed earlier.

(Continued)

1. Is Patrick responding to Mary in ways similar to significant others in the past (complementary countertransference)?
2. Does Patrick's countertransference relate to his personal issues and sensitivities (subjective countertransference)?
3. Is Patrick feeling like Mary is feeling now in therapy or has often felt in the past (concordant countertransference)?

Applying these questions, which of the above do you think best fits Patrick's countertransference and was there evidence of more than one type of countertransference reaction, in your opinion?

Step Four: Managing the countertransference reactions

In Chapters 5 and 6, we discuss issues related to managing countertransference in more depth. In the remainder of this chapter, we will look briefly at how Patrick can work on managing his reactions in a way that is helpful for the client and therapy.

At this point, it is also important to recall that the previous steps – being aware of and conceptualising the countertransference reactions – are all designed to help manage countertransference reactions. Working through these steps puts the therapist in a stronger position to manage these reactions well. Then when therapists experience countertransference reactions in therapy sessions it is helpful to focus initially on containing these reactions – that is, recognising the reactions (the thoughts, feelings, urges, images, bodily sensations), experiencing them, but not acting on them.

CONTAINING THE COUNTERTRANSFERENCE

It would be hurtful for Mary and confirm her negative representations of self and other/s if Patrick became annoyed or acted in a way that she experienced as being pushed away by him. Patrick could withdraw and cut off from her emotionally as he struggled with his feelings or he could become annoyed and speak to her in a sharp tone or with an annoyed look on his face. He could make an interpretation that she would experience as a put-down, such as, 'I'm wondering if this is the kind of neediness that you get into in relationships with others that led them to push you away'. There may be times in the future that Patrick will help Mary reflect on what she contributes to her relationship problems but this is not the time to do it and it has to be done much more sensitively and without any aggressive urges.

Although it may be less likely, Patrick could also shift into a nurturing type of parent role in order to avoid becoming a bad other, and could talk about the possibility of making an exception for her, offering her phone or zoom sessions when he is away. This might be a viable option in some instances but this break in therapy was negotiated with Mary, and Patrick making an exception could also be experienced by Mary as confirmation that she is a particularly needy person. Patrick may also need this time for himself. And what has arisen in session – Mary's neediness and desperation – is what brought her to therapy, so this is an opportunity for Patrick to fully understand Mary's experience and assist her with this. Hence, initially, Patrick needs to experience and also contain the emotional reaction while not being reactive but at the same time remain responsive to Mary.

USING A CALMING STRATEGY

It is helpful for therapists to be conscious of their breathing and to take some deep breaths and to engage in calming thoughts. Patrick could say to himself: 'I am having a countertransference reaction. I don't really understand it at this point but I can think about it later. I can take some deep breaths and stay calm'. Therapists who practise mindfulness and meditation will be able to use the strategies they have developed as part of these practices. Personally, I also found it helpful to learn a deep-breathing technique and to practise it throughout the day, so that when I needed to use it – in a stressful or demanding situation – I could shift into doing that form of breathing in order to calm and centre myself.

MOVING BACK INTO THE ADULT

Another strategy that works for some people is to encourage or coach themselves back into the Adult self. Patrick might prefer to refer to this as his Wise self or his Wise Therapist self. He could say something such as: 'I have experienced this countertransference. I can now move back into my Adult self'. The adult self can also make sense of the countertransference reaction. See Figure 3.4 for a representation of moving back into the Adult.

TAKING AN EMPATHIC POSITION

Taking an empathic position towards the client can also assist the therapist to move back into the Adult. Patrick, for example, could say to himself: 'Mary is distressed and she is doing the best she can' or 'My going away might be triggering Mary. It may be triggering emotions associated with all of the times that her parents went away and she felt left out. It might also be bringing out the sense of desperation she felt then. It's important for me to be calm and empathic'. Remaining calm and showing acceptance and empathy for Mary may also help her to calm down and feel more centred.

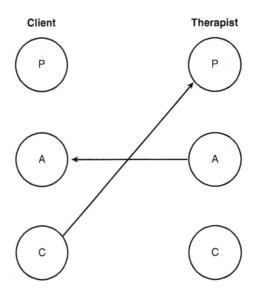

Figure 3.4 Moving back into the Adult

The other side of the coin is that therapists need to also have empathy for them-selves. Just as Mary is acting out from the hurt and sense of rejection she has experienced in her life, so too Patrick's own hurts or wounds have been trig-gered. This does not undermine Patrick as a therapist, as long as he can recog-nise this in himself. Potentially, it can make him a more empathic therapist.

TALKING WITH THE CLIENT ABOUT WHAT IS HAPPENING FOR THEM

We will discuss managing therapeutic disruptions or ruptures in much more depth in Chapter 5. As therapists from many persuasions believe, times like this in therapy where there is some tension between therapist and client are important as they often link to themes that are central to clients' lives and are associated with emotional pain. However, getting through a time like this in therapy can help to strengthen the therapeutic relationship and learning can occur. Having observed Mary's distress and having made sense of his countertransference reaction, Patrick can talk to Mary about how she is feeling about him going away, and he can give her some support with this. Patrick could say, 'Mary, I just noticed that you became a little worried or upset when I mentioned my going away for the two weeks. Can you tell me how you are feeling about that?'. If Mary denies she has been triggered by this, then Patrick can help to normalise this for her, 'It would be OK if you were feeling concerned about us not having sessions for two weeks. Clients sometimes find breaks in therapy hard, especially once they have started talking about the really important things in their lives'. If Mary is able to say she is worried, upset, or even angry, then Patrick can also respond empathically to this and they can, for example, explore her worries and find new ways to manage them over the next few weeks.

Managing countertransference and the four steps

In this chapter, I have presented the four steps to conceptualising and managing countertransference as if they are consecutive. However, often in therapy sessions, we have to respond to what is happening for the client and how they are relating to us in the moment. We cannot take 10 minutes out to reflect on it. For someone learning about countertransference, it can be helpful initially to focus on recognising and containing your countertransference reactions, and moving back into the Adult or Wise Therapist position. It works well to then reflect on the interactions with your clients and your countertransference responses with a clinical supervisor or colleagues. Gradually, however, you will be able to go through all these steps in session. For myself, I have the three questions that I consider, in the moment, to help me figure out what might be happening.

1. Am I responding to the client as significant others have? (Complementary)
2. Am I feeling like the client is feeling now in therapy or has often felt in the past? (Concordant)
3. Is my countertransference related to my own personal issues and sensitivities? (Subjective)

Pause and reflect: The therapist's self–other representations

At this point, it will be useful for you to reflect on your own self–other representations. A way to access this is to think about the main types of emotional-cognitive states that you shift into in everyday life. This could include feeling anxious and submissive with people whom you perceive as dominant, feeling really excited when you get praise, feeling hurt and rejecting towards people who disagree with you, and so on. These reactions are manifestations, if you like, of the self–other representations that underlie your patterns of relationships.

It may also help to think about the themes that have emerged for you in your relationships, beginning importantly with childhood ones, and through to current times. You might also think about any sensitivities you have noticed in yourself in your relationships with clients, that is, what triggers you.

(Continued)

> You can then propose for yourself the self–other representations that you hold and that influence how you respond to others. As you read this book, you can continue to reflect on these representations and you may change or refine them. Talking through this with your therapist, if you are in therapy, might also be helpful.

At the end of this chapter is a reflective practice guide that provides an overview of the four-step process. This can be used to guide reflective practice in relation to countertransference. As will be discussed in later chapters, engaging in regular reflective practice in relation to countertransference may increase awareness of our reactions and the ability to conceptualise what is happening in session, which can in turn assist in managing counter-transference reactions.

Summary

This chapter presented the four-step approach to conceptualising and managing countertransference, and the concepts that are used in this approach. The first step emphasises the importance of attending to and having awareness of countertransference reactions as they arise in therapy sessions. The second step focuses on understanding the relational patterns of the client in order to better understand the ways in which they respond to the therapist in sessions. The concept of self–other representations is used in this step, and therapists are also encouraged to develop a conceptualisation of their own self–other representations and patterns of relating to others.

The third step integrates the understanding of the relational patterns of the client developed in Step two with the use of the PAC model to trace out the patterns of interaction as they occur in therapy sessions. This allows the therapist to consider the client's transference (if this is relevant) and the therapist's countertransference. The fourth step is managing the countertransference reaction. This includes being able to experience and contain the emotional reaction without acting/speaking on it, using self-calming strategies if needed, taking an empathic position towards the client, moving back into the Adult or Wise Therapist self. Strategies for managing countertransference, including talking to clients about what is happening in therapy, were briefly discussed and will be discussed in further depth in Chapters 5 and 6.

Reflective practice guide

Step One: Monitoring and being aware of your countertransference responses

- Which countertransference response/s would you like to consider?
- Describe your reaction/s and what was happening in therapy when you felt like this?
- What was happening for the client?

Step Two: Reflecting on the client's patterns of relating to others

- What are the client's self–other representations and which of these might be coming out in therapy in the way that they are relating to you?
- Was there anything in this situation that was personally triggering for you?

Step Three: Using the PAC model and self–other representations to reflect on the interpersonal processes

Use the PAC model (see Figure 3.5) to reflect on your countertransference and how it emerged out of your interactions with the client.

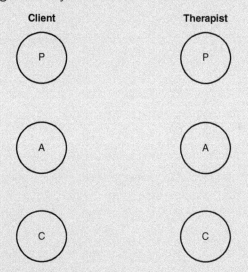

Figure 3.5   Blank PAC model

- What, if any, self–other representations were triggered for the client (and the therapist) during the interactions?
- What are your hypotheses about the interpersonal processes between yourself and the client at this time?

Step Four: Managing the countertransference reaction

- How did you manage the countertransference reaction during the session?
- What if anything would you like to do differently next time?

Recommended readings

Bateman, A., Brown, B., & Pedder, J. (2000). *An introduction to psychotherapy: An outline of psychodynamic principles and practices.* London, UK: Routledge.

Cartwright, C., Rhodes, P., King, R., & Shires, A. (2015). A pilot study of a method for teaching clinical psychology trainees to conceptualise and manage countertransference. *Australian Psychologist, 50,* 148–156.

Miranda, R. & Andersen, S. (2007). The therapeutic relationship: Implications for cognition and transference. In P. Gilbert and R. Leahy (Eds.), *The therapeutic relationship in the cognitive behavioral psychotherapies* (pp. 63–69). New York, NY: Routledge.

Newman, C. (2013). *Core competencies in Cognitive-Behavioral Therapy.* New York, NY: Routledge.

4

Understanding Countertransference in Practice

This chapter aims to deepen understanding of the four-step approach and especially the second and third steps that focus on understanding the client's (and therapist's) templates for relationships (self–other representations) and the interpersonal processes, including transference and countertransference, that arise in therapy sessions. In this chapter, we will apply the approach to a new case study and reflect on this case from two perspectives – a psychodynamic perspective and a CBT perspective. In the final part of the chapter, we will also think about events in Mary and Patrick's therapeutic relationship (Chapter 3) from a CBT perspective.

The case below presents Eddie who has come for assistance with social anxiety and panic attacks that appear to be associated with social and performance situations.

Case study: Eddie and Angeline

Eddie, 30 years old, was referred to a therapist, Angeline, by his general practitioner for help with anxiety and panic attacks. Angeline realised after meeting Eddie that she had been expecting someone who was quite anxious. Instead, Eddie presented as confident and relaxed. He appeared to be happy to be there, and talked about his anxiety and panic attacks as if they were really quite minor. It became clear though over the first two sessions that his anxiety was seriously interfering with his work and also social situations. He was avoiding situations that triggered his anxiety and this was putting him in difficult situations at work and also with friends.

Angeline and Eddie had 20 therapy sessions together and when these sessions ended, Eddie had learnt strategies for managing his anxiety and panic attacks and had not had any for two months. Angeline and Eddie had also gotten to what Angeline thought of as the main origins of his panic and social anxiety – the events that had occurred in Eddie's childhood that he had been attempting to repress. By the time sessions ended, he appeared to have insight into the impact of these childhood experiences on him and their relationship to his social anxiety and his panic attacks. He was also more forgiving of himself and kinder to himself.

In the early sessions, Angeline had attempted to gain an understanding of Eddie's developmental history, as she usually did. However, talking about his childhood appeared to be difficult for Eddie. When she asked about growing up, he tended to respond with short answers, mainly generalisations such as 'It was alright growing up', 'It was just a normal childhood', 'Typical child'. He also appeared to get irritated with Angeline if she asked for more detail, and acted as if his childhood was irrelevant and she was wasting his time. When this happened, Angeline had a sense of a wall going up between them and also felt twinges of hurt and fear.

Despite this, Angeline did ask about Eddie's childhood experiences. She checked to see if he had experienced any type of abuse as a child, and he said no. She asked him about his relationships with his mother, his father, and his place in the family. She asked him about how he had found school and about his friendships and relationships with teachers. On one occasion, he talked about being a 'cry baby as a kid' and said that his father couldn't stand it when he cried, and his mother did nothing but say 'There, there'. School he said was 'fine', 'OK', 'normal'.

After making these statements, he appeared to shut down again. He looked irritated and seemed to withdraw into himself. Once again, Angeline had a sense of a wall coming up between them and felt a bit fearful and hurt. In order to try to understand what was happening for Eddie, Angeline commented that she had noticed that he appeared to find it difficult and perhaps was a little annoyed with her when she asked about his childhood, and Eddie said, 'It's just a waste of time. There's nothing to worry about. It's what's happening now that I need help with. I don't want to dwell on the past'.

Eddie also became more engaged when they focused on the present, his panic attacks, and how he was managing work and social situations. At these times, Eddie appeared to have become more open and more comfortable talking and was making use of the sessions and developing strategies for managing his anxiety. On the other hand, Angeline thought that, despite the unspoken no-go messages, she needed to find a way that would facilitate Eddie to open up – if there was something there. She felt that she had to try at least one more time.

One day this conversation took place:

Angeline: Eddie, can you think of anything that has happened to you in the past that might be still affecting you – that might underlie your sense of feeling unsafe around others?

Eddie: Oh for God's sake. Is it because I am messed up that you think I must have had a screwed-up past?!! [Eddie appeared angry and raised his voice]

Angeline: [Pause] Not at all Eddie. Have you been feeling like that – that I think you are messed up? [Pause] Have I done or said some things to lead you to feel like that?

Eddie: [Pause] Not really. But I don't want to talk about my past.

[Angeline notes that this is the first time that Eddie has said this directly and this seems to confirm that he is avoiding talking about something important. She also thinks that she will need to come back to the issue that Eddie has raised about her attitude towards him being messed up, but decides to leave this for now]

Angeline: You know Eddie, it's quite common and it's normal to not want to talk about difficult things that have happened in the past, but my concern for you is this – if something happened to you, and the memories and the effects of that are contributing to the fear you feel around people, then I'm concerned that if you keep it to yourself and don't talk about it, then it will continue to affect you and undermine you in your life. This is why I am bringing it up. I feel like I wouldn't be doing right by you if I didn't talk about this with you.

Eddie: [Sighs] You're bloody persistent.

Angeline: You seem to be suggesting that there is something. Can you tell me what you are worried might happen if you talk to me about it?

Eddie: It will mean I am a pathetic wimp. [Eddie hung his head and looked deflated]

Angeline: Really? Something happened to you and it leads you to feel like a pathetic wimp?

Eddie: [Long pause] Yes.

Following a long pause, Eddie begins to tell Angeline about the bullying he experienced between the ages of 8 and 9. He only tells her a little but over the next three sessions it becomes clear that the bullying was serious and terrifying for Eddie. A group of three older boys around the age of 11 and 12 bullied him regularly over a one-year period. They waited for him after school and came out from behind school buildings and attacked him physically, punching him in places where bruises wouldn't show. They called him names like sissy, dickhead, fuckwit, and said he was a pathetic wimp. Three or four times they locked him in a small dark shed on the school grounds for several hours. They dragged him there and he was in the dark, terrified he wouldn't be found. He recalls that they bullied him at least once every two or three weeks, and they put him in the shed four or five times, for hours. He never knew when it was going to happen. One of them told him if he called out for help or told anyone, they would kill him. It ended when the boy who was the 'ring-leader' was expelled from school for bullying another child. Eddie had never spoken to anyone about this before, although it was around this time that he became a 'pathetic cry-baby' at home and his father became angry and critical of him. In response to Angeline's questions, Eddie said he had been 'terrified' and 'humiliated' by the bullying. He also felt very hurt and kept wondering, 'Why me?'. He felt like everybody knew what a 'pathetic wimp' he was and saw that 'something was wrong' with him. When he reached teenage years and became tall, he decided to put it behind him and act strong and become strong – 'If I let it affect me, then I am a wimp'.

Over the sessions in which Eddie gradually revealed more of his experiences, Angeline had a sense that Eddie's feelings towards her shifted at different times and hers towards Eddie. At times, it felt like their therapeutic alliance was strong and they were putting their heads (and hearts) together to work through what had happened to Eddie and how it had affected him. At other times, it felt like Eddie resented her, as if she were causing him this pain and it would have been better if he had never spoken about it. He appeared to get angry at Angeline and withdraw. At these times, Angeline felt hurt and rejected, although she tried to contain and make sense of these feelings. At other times, Eddie seemed to get in touch with his hurt Child and on two occasions broke down and cried about what had happened to him. Angeline felt a lot of compassion for Eddie. After this, again he seemed to Angeline to be a bit resentful towards her, although this shifted again to feeling like he was experiencing her as empathic and helpful.

Step Two: Reflecting on the client's patterns of relating to others

It appears that Eddie has problematic self–other representations that impact on his life. The effects of the bullying, his father's disapproval of him being a 'cry-baby', his parents' inability to support him when they did not know what was happening, and the way in which he distanced himself from others in keeping the secret of the bullying to himself will all have contributed to his fears in social situations and his problematic views of self and others.

He has described himself as a 'pathetic wimp', a 'pathetic cry-baby', and as having 'something wrong' with him that is visible to others. He was 'terrified' and 'humiliated' by the bullying, and he was also 'hurt' – emotionally and physically.

The value of relevant research and clinical literature

It is helpful to remember to turn to our research and clinical literature to help us understand our clients' experiences and their views of self and other. Eddie has been a victim of bullying. A number of studies have looked at the long-term impacts of bullying; and the literature on surviving child abuse might also be helpful in understanding Eddie. DeLara (2019), for example, interviewed 72 young adults who had been bullied as children. In this study, childhood or adolescent bullying resulted in ongoing problems for some participants including social anxiety, recurrent sadness or depression, shame, rage, fantasies of revenge, and for some, suicidal behaviour. Shame was particularly associated with being victimised and name-calling. Participants also reported problems in friendships and relationships, and difficulty in trusting themselves and others.

Eddie's self and other representations

Based on our understanding of Eddie and how he has talked about himself and others, I propose that Eddie has a representation of *self as weak/victimised* and *others as unsafe/unpredictable*. He also appears to have a representation of *self as having something wrong with him* and representations of *other/s as judgmental/critical or hurtful/wounding*. Feelings of anxiety, fear, humiliation or shame, hurt, and perhaps self-blame, appear to be associated with these self–other representations.

USING THE PAC MODEL TO REFLECT ON EDDIE'S INTERNAL PROCESSES

One of the areas that we have not discussed up until now is the way in which the PAC model can be used to reflect on the individual's internal (or intrapersonal) processes. We can use the PAC model to reflect on Eddie's self–other representations and his Parent, Adult, and Child states. See Figure 4.1.

We can think of Eddie as having a frightened and hurt Child and one that fears future victimisation. He may also have a critical Parent that thinks that the hurt Child part of him is a 'pathetic wimp'. Eddie's Parent has been pretty tough on his Child – he has not allowed his vulnerable Child any expression and he has not allowed himself to seek any support. The experience of being in the Child and the vulnerability associated with that may feel aversive for Eddie. The memories of the bullying may evoke emotions that feel unbearable. Hence, Eddie has repressed his vulnerable Child aspects. When an external trigger (a sudden movement, a type of laughter, or his therapist's questions) or internal trigger (a memory from his past) evokes the vulnerable Child aspect, Eddie may shift into his Parental self – he could be critical of himself, 'Stop being a wimp. Get over it' or he could be a kind and nurturing Parent to himself,

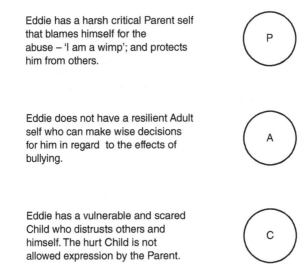

Eddie has a harsh critical Parent self that blames himself for the abuse – 'I am a wimp'; and protects him from others.

Eddie does not have a resilient Adult self who can make wise decisions for him in regard to the effects of bullying.

Eddie has a vulnerable and scared Child who distrusts others and himself. The hurt Child is not allowed expression by the Parent.

Figure 4.1 A representation of Eddie's Parent, Adult, and Child

'It's OK. It's safe. Stay calm'. At the beginning of therapy, however, Eddie did not appear to have a well-developed nurturing Parent nor an Adult self that could understand them. Thinking about Eddie's internal processes using the PAC model will also help us to think about what is happening for Eddie as he relates to his therapist.

In the next section, we will reflect on the interpersonal processes between Eddie and Angeline as they occurred in the sessions described above. Before doing so, we can consider Angeline's reaction to Eddie.

Pause and reflect: Subjective countertransference

We always need to consider subjective or personal countertransference. A therapist in Angeline's situation may have some particular sensitivities that will contribute to her countertransference reactions to Eddie, and to her therapeutic decisions and interventions, for example, if therapists have experienced some form of bullying or abuse as children, or engaged in some bullying themselves, they may find their own memories and emotions are triggered by hearing about others' experiences, which in turn make it difficult to be confident in how to respond to the client. Therapists who have experienced secrecy or denial of problems within their families as children may also struggle with the balance between supporting and challenging the client who denies or withholds their experiences and thoughts and feelings from the therapist.

Can you think of any other therapist sensitivities or unresolved issues that could be triggered in working with a client with Eddie's problems and ways of responding?

Step Three: Developing hypotheses about the interpersonal processes

When the client gives a no-go message

In this step, we are going to focus initially on Eddie's transference and Angeline's countertransference during the times when Angeline felt that she was receiving a 'no-go' message from Eddie. This tended to happen whenever she shifted to talking about or asking Eddie about his childhood or past experiences. She felt some anxiety as she approached this topic. She then had a sense of a wall going down between them and Eddie appeared to become angry with her and to withdraw. She felt twinges of fear and hurt.

We could just think of this in lay-person's terms – the therapist was not responding to Eddie's message to leave the topic alone and he was rightfully annoyed about it and the therapist was a bit frightened and hurt by his response. The other possibility is that Angeline's questions about his childhood triggered a representation of other as hurtful/abusive and of self as hurt and victimised. This led Eddie to shift into his vulnerable Child and then into his critical Adult towards the therapist. Angeline felt hurt and fearful. This suggests that she shifted into a vulnerable Child position, experiencing a concordant countertransference.

Figure 4.2 shows two different representations for this concordant countertransference. In a concordant countertransference, the therapist identifies with a self-representation (or Child self) of the client. Concordant countertransference

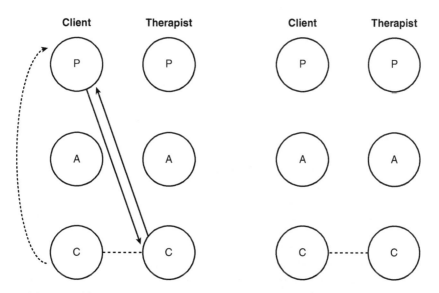

Figure 4.2   Two PAC model representations of a concordant countertransference

is in some ways similar to empathy. When we experience a concordant counter-transference, we are experiencing something akin to what the client is experiencing or what the client has often experienced in life.

In Figure 4.2, the PAC model on the left represents Eddie shifting into his vulnerable Child when asked about his past, and then shifting into his critical Parent (dotted line), perhaps as a defence against his vulnerability. He then responds to Angeline in an angry and critical way. Angeline shifts into a Child self, feeling fear and hurt, thus identifying with Eddie's vulnerable Child. The representation on the right simply represents the final concordant countertransference position in which Angeline identifies with Eddie's vulnerable Child.

Concordant countertransference

I find that trainee and beginning therapists often identify with their countertransference reactions. It feels as if the countertransference is about them and nothing to do with the client. It is common, for example, for a trainee to feel down, hopeless, and helpless with a deeply depressed and stuck client. Sometimes trainees describe feeling exhausted and going home exhausted. Some describe having to rest or sleep. Trainees become convinced that they are hopeless in this context. They begin thinking that they lack experience, are incompetent beginners, and cannot help such a depressed person. When I introduce the idea of a concordant countertransference to trainees, they are often polite but somewhat disbelieving. However, over time, when trainees accept that this is a possibility – that they may be experiencing something similar to what the client is experiencing or identifying with the client's emotional reactions – this becomes a source of insight for them and helps them to take the fourth step and find a way of getting back into the Adult.

Talking through the experiences of being bullied

We will now consider what might have been happening between Eddie and Angeline when the therapist felt Eddie's anger and withdrawal towards her during therapy sessions in which they talked about the bullying and its effect on him. One of the strategies that appears to be helpful for clients who have experienced traumatic experiences is to talk about and face into these experiences. However, this can be a difficult process and it is helpful for therapist and client to have developed a good therapeutic alliance before this stage of therapy.

When therapists encourage clients to face into traumatic memories, clients can feel that the therapist is causing or provoking their pain. In this way, the therapist can be experienced as a hurtful person or even as an abuser. When Angeline encouraged Eddie to talk through some of his specific memories, the emotions associated with those memories may have been triggered. It seems likely that Eddie's representation of other as abusive and causing hurt may have also been triggered and transferred to Angeline. Angeline recalled feeling hurt, fearful, and a sense of being rejected at these times – almost as if Eddie had become a hurtful and rejecting person towards Angeline. This is similar to Angeline's concordant countertransference during the 'no-go' interactions that are represented in Figure 4.2. As Angeline experiences the feelings of hurt, rejecting, and fear, she can wonder if these are akin to the feelings that Eddie has carried in his life, and also in sessions when he is fearful of opening up and talking about his past. The PAC model on the right of Figure 4.2 can represent the process by which the therapist, Angeline, identifies with Eddie's emotional experience.

A cognitive-behavioural perspective

In this section, we will reflect again on Eddie's transference and Angeline's countertransference but this time from a CBT perspective. In Chapter 1, we briefly examined the ways in which some expert CBT therapists view counter-transference and the terminology they use when discussing these therapist reactions. Prior to reflecting on Eddie and Angeline's transference and countertransference reactions, we will revisit these ideas and also review CBT concepts that are relevant to understanding transference and countertransference from a CBT perspective.

Understanding countertransference within a CBT framework

Aaron Beck, regarded as the founder of CT and CBT, was originally a psychoanalyst and therefore had a deep understanding of the psychoanalytic concepts of transference and countertransference. He and his colleagues acknowledged the importance of transference and countertransference in their text on working with personality disorders (Beck et al., 2004). They expressed a preference, however, for referring to these processes as client and therapist emotional reactions. Client transferences or emotional reactions to therapists could be viewed in CBT terms as resulting from the overgeneralised beliefs, expectations, and assumptions that clients hold about themselves, others, and relationships. Understanding these emotional reactions and the belief systems that underlie the reactions is central to CBT. The centrality of emotions in CBT is demonstrated by the title of one of Beck's first books – *Cognitive Therapy and the Emotional Disorders*.

While transference can be viewed as resulting from the overgeneralised beliefs about self, others, and relationships, countertransference can be viewed as the therapist's normative emotional reactions to the client (Newman, 2013). In other words, the therapist is responding in similar ways as others do in the client's daily life. The therapist's emotional reactions as normative to the client's way of relating has similarities to what we have discussed previously as objective countertransference.

On the other hand, as Leahy (2007) notes, therapist emotional reactions to clients can also result from the therapists' own beliefs, expectations, and assumptions about self, others, and relationships that underlie their ways of relating to others. This is similar to what we have discussed previously as subjective or personal countertransference. And it seems likely that some, if not many, of our emotional reactions to clients are normative reactions to clients' systems of belief about self, others, and their patterns of behaving in relationships, and are also based on our own system of beliefs and patterns of relationships.

While CBT therapists focus on conscious processes rather than unconscious ones, they also believe that individuals are often not aware of the thoughts and beliefs that are motivating them at any moment in time. CBT aims to increase awareness of the problematic thoughts and beliefs that underlie the presenting problems.

Relevant CBT concepts

CBT approaches place emphasis on understanding the problematic cognitions (thoughts and beliefs) that underlie the client's presenting problems. Commonly, CBT therapists reflect on three levels of cognitions when formulating the client's problems. These include the core beliefs or schema about self, others, relationships, the world, and the future; intermediate beliefs (such as conditional assumptions and rules); and automatic thoughts (e.g., Beck, 2011; Newman, 2013). Core beliefs are deep-seated beliefs that a person holds about himself, others, relationships, and the world. These beliefs are the person's truths – what we really believe deep down inside. These core beliefs, when activated, can be associated with distressing emotions that are overwhelming or difficult to manage. Core beliefs are developed mainly through formative childhood experiences. In clients with personality disorders, core beliefs are rigidly held and are very problematic for them.

Intermediate beliefs are developed to cope with the core beliefs as they influence and operate in everyday life. For example, a young child who has experienced a lack of interest and care by parents and/or others in the family may develop a core belief that they are unlovable. The child may develop a conditional assumption that might help them to cope with the undermining core belief, such as, 'If am undemanding and act kind to others then others may accept me' or a rule, 'I should be kind and undemanding of others' or 'I should never express anger at others'.

The third level of belief refers to the automatic thoughts. These are the thoughts that are running through our minds during our daily lives – evaluative thoughts about ourselves, other people, events in our day as they unfold, our ruminations, and so on. These thoughts occur spontaneously and have a significant influence on how we are feeling and what we do.

Aaron Beck observed a negative stream of thoughts that depressed clients were experiencing about themselves and their lives when he was working as a psychoanalyst. He named these automatic thoughts or negative automatic thoughts (NATs). We are not always aware of our automatic thoughts although we can become aware of them quite easily if we attend to them. This is one of the key therapy interventions that CBT therapists engage in – helping clients to become aware of and question their problematic automatic thoughts and to consider more realistic or adaptive ones. Our automatic thoughts, both positive and negative, can be viewed as manifestations of our core beliefs or schemas. Therefore, if people are able to change their automatic thoughts over time to more adaptive thoughts, then this may lead to a weakening of negative core beliefs about self and about others.

CBT therapists also talk about the five-part model and some use this to help clients reflect on their reactions to events. The five parts include the environment or the context for the reaction, the automatic thoughts that are triggered by the current event/s, the emotions that these thoughts evoke, the person's physiological reaction, and the person's behavioural response.

In the next section, we will reflect on Eddie's transference and Angeline's countertransference using these CBT concepts. As discussed in Chapter 1, some CBT therapists may use the term countertransference although it may be more common to use the term therapist emotions rather than countertransference. In this section, I will use the term client and therapist emotions.

This chapter is focusing on understanding countertransference in practice and up until now has focussed on Steps Two and Three of the four-step model. However, in this section I will also briefly discuss Steps One and Four from a CBT perspective. The titles of these steps are adapted to fit with the CBT perspective.

Step One: Monitoring emotions in therapy

Understanding clients' emotional reactions in therapy is central to therapeutic activities. It is also vital for us to monitor our own emotional reactions. These reactions can be normative reactions to clients' interpersonal styles and/or can be related to the therapist's personal beliefs. There is a risk that therapist emotions can lead to therapists engaging in therapy-interfering behaviours (just as clients' emotions can). Monitoring and being aware of our emotional responses is the first step in managing any such therapist behaviours.

Angeline first became aware of what she thought of as Eddie's No-Go messages early on in their sessions when she first asked about his childhood experiences. Eddie's reaction to her asking about his childhood seemed to become a little stronger each time she asked. She observed Eddie becoming anxious, looking angry, looking down at the floor, becoming less communicative. She also had the feeling of a wall coming down between them. Angeline herself felt some anxiety, hurt, and anger. She had to focus on remaining calm.

Step Two: Reflecting on the client's thoughts and beliefs

In this step, we will reflect on Eddie's thoughts and beliefs (core and intermediate beliefs, and automatic thoughts) that may have been activated in these therapy situations. Eddie is likely to have developed negative core beliefs about himself and others based on his childhood experiences of being bullied, his father's criticism, his lack of support (his parents were unaware of the bullying), and being distanced from others by his secret. I hypothesise that Eddie's core beliefs are that he is *weak* and *there is something wrong* with him. Core beliefs about others seem to be that others are *unsafe* or *unpredictable*, *judgmental*, and/or *hurtful*. The emotions that Eddie experiences when his core beliefs are triggered include anxiety/fear, hurt, anger, and self-blame and perhaps shame, as suggested by his statement, 'I'm a pathetic wimp'. These beliefs of himself as weak and having something wrong with him and his core beliefs that others are unsafe, unpredictable, and judgmental are likely to be perpetuating his panic attacks.

Eddie appears to have an assumption that if he does not allow himself to be affected by the abuse then he is not a 'pathetic wimp'. Eddie appears to have adopted a rule (an intermediate belief) for himself that he must never talk about the bullying he experienced. He has kept to this rule throughout his life and avoided talking about the bullying to the therapist. He also appears to have an assumption that if he does not talk about the bullying, he will be OK and will not be seen as weak and as having something wrong with him. If he is not affected by the bullying, then he is not a 'pathetic wimp'. In this way, others will not see his vulnerability and will instead view him as OK.

In terms of his coping strategies Eddie appears to engage in cognitive avoidance – that is, he tries not to think about the abuse he experienced. He also engages in experiential avoidance – he does not want to experience the emotions that are inevitably evoked by the memories of the abuse. These avoidances act as therapy-interfering behaviours, although they can be viewed as functional within

Eddie's beliefs – Hypotheses

Core beliefs about self: I am weak. There is something wrong with me.

Core beliefs about others: Others are unsafe/unpredictable. Others are judgmental and/or hurtful.

Intermediate beliefs: I must never tell anyone what happened to me (rule); If I don't tell anyone, they won't know I am a wimp (assumption); If I'm not affected by it, then I am in control (assumption).

Coping strategies: Cognitive avoidance – don't let myself think about what happened; experiential avoidance – avoid negative emotions and memories.

the structure that his core beliefs of self and others, and his intermediate beliefs allow.

Step Three: Hypotheses about the interpersonal processes

We can now reflect on Eddie's emotional reactions to Angeline and Angeline's emotional reactions to Eddie in the No-Go therapy situations. Eddie has come to therapy because his panic attacks are interfering significantly with his life. When Angeline is working with Eddie on his panic attacks and when he is getting some relief from his anxiety symptoms Eddie appears to have a positive working alliance with Angeline. However, when Angeline asks about his childhood, Eddie becomes withdrawn, angry, and withdraws from Angeline, as discussed previously. We can make use of the cognitive-behavioural formulation presented above to understand Eddie's reactions in these situations.

Eddie's emotional reactions to Angeline during the No-Go events

It appears likely that Eddie's core and intermediate beliefs were triggered whenever Angeline asked him about his childhood. When Eddie's core beliefs of self as weak and having something wrong with him were triggered so too were his core beliefs of others as unpredictable/hurtful/judgmental. He also experienced the emotions associated with these beliefs including fear, hurt, shame, and also anger towards the therapist.

We can use the five-part model to reflect further on Eddie's emotional reactions during these interactions. The triggering event appears to be Angeline asking a question about his past experiences. This activated negative automatic thoughts that linked to his beliefs about self and others, such as, 'She thinks I am messed up, why is she dwelling on this?'. The NATs could also reflect Eddie's intermediate beliefs ('I should not talk about this; and she should not ask'). His emotional reactions appeared to be fear, anger, and perhaps hurt. He was uptight and he made an angry remark and then gave the impression of withdrawing.

Reflecting on Eddie's reactions to the therapist using the five-part model

Trigger: Therapist asks a question about his past experiences.

Automatic negative thoughts: I should not talk about this. I don't want to dwell on the past. I've let her know I don't want to talk about it. She shouldn't keep asking.

Emotions: Frightened, angry, perhaps hurt.

Physiological: Tense, state of hyperarousal.

Behaviours: Angry remark, withdrawal.

Hence, Eddie's reactions towards Angeline can be conceptualised based on a CBT formulation of Eddie's presenting problems.

Angeline's emotions in therapy

As discussed in Chapter 1, therapists' emotional reactions can be in response to the clients' reactions towards their therapists. However, therapists' reactions to clients can also relate to their own core and intermediate beliefs. We shall consider both of these possibilities below.

Angeline felt she received a No-Go message from Eddie in relation to discussing his past. She had a sense of 'a wall going up' between her and Eddie on the occasions that she asked about his childhood experience. Eddie appeared to become annoyed with her and also to withdraw from interacting with her. When Eddie responded like this Angeline felt anxious and noticed twinges of fear and feeling hurt.

A NORMATIVE RESPONSE

Angeline's emotional response to Eddie's No-Go reactions can be seen as a normative response. Her reactions may be similar to those of others in Eddie's life and reflective of the impact that Eddie has on others when his negative belief system is activated. During the No-Go events, Eddie responds to Angeline as if she is hurtful, uncaring or untrustworthy. Angeline's emotions of anxiety, fear, and hurt can be seen as normative responses to Eddie's negative reactions to her. This provides her with some insight into how Eddie might respond to others when his buttons are pushed and how others might feel in response. Eddie's reaction is also a source of information for Angeline. She can think about what his reactions mean – what beliefs and meaning have been activated for Eddie at these moments?

A PERSONAL RESPONSE

On the other hand, we have to consider if Angeline's emotional reactions to Eddie's emotional responses are based on her own maladaptive beliefs. It is possible that Angeline's own core and/or intermediate beliefs, and coping strategies are contributing to her emotional reactions to Eddie. For example, Angeline could hold a belief that she must not cause distress to clients and particularly to vulnerable clients. Alternatively she could find client disapproval difficult if she has had a history of feeling disapproved of by important early others. Neither of these seem to fit Angeline, however, as she persists with encouraging Eddie to talk about his past and his formative experiences.

Hopefully, Angeline has developed a formulation of her own system of beliefs and coping strategies. This will help her in working out how much of her reactions to Eddie are personal to her.

Managing emotions in therapy

This current chapter focuses on understanding countertransference in practice. Managing countertransference in practice is the focus of Chapters 5 and 6. However, it seems important to write briefly here about managing therapist emotional reactions in CBT therapy.

CBT places emphasis on a collaborative relationship between therapist and client. CBT approaches also emphasise the importance of therapists maintaining non-judgmental and warm attitudes towards clients even if the clients are challenging or provocative. Judith Beck (2011), for example, talks about her commitment to striving to demonstrate 'warmth, empathy, caring, genuine regard and competence' (p. 8). (We can think of this as being similar to therapists remaining and attempting to be in their Adult selves, as discussed previously.)

CBT strategies, such as thought records, can be used by CBT therapists to assist with developing awareness of the automatic thoughts and beliefs triggered in therapeutic contexts in order to manage these emotions and reduce the risk of therapy-interfering behaviours. Therapists, like clients, are not always aware of the automatic thoughts they experience in therapy. Step One emphasises the importance of monitoring our emotions. Step Four emphasises the importance of revealing these thoughts and beliefs that are leading to the emotional reactions in order to better challenge these as they arise. Other strategies, such as those discussed in Chapter 3 can be employed by the CBT therapist. Therapists can engage in helpful self-talk or calming thoughts, practice calming strategies, and practise maintaining a non-judgmental and caring attitude.

In the next chapter, we will turn to thinking more about how therapists can manage periods of disruptions or rupture to the therapeutic relationship and therapeutic alliance, such as the ones we have been discussing with Eddie and Angeline. Before doing so, however, some readers might find it helpful to practise reflecting on another case, using a CBT perspective. This is the case of Mary and Patrick discussed in Chapter 3 (pp. 48–56).

Developing a CBT formulation of client and therapist emotions in therapy

Prior to beginning this exercise, you may wish to re-read the background information on therapy between Mary and Patrick. Once you have familiarised yourself with this, you can complete the reflective practice exercises below.

I will then briefly present my CBT analysis of Mary and Patrick's emotional reactions in therapy.

> ### Pause and reflect: Developing a CBT formulation for Mary
>
> CBT practitioners often develop tentative formulations of clients' presenting problems and these are continually assessed and adapted to better account for clients' experiences.
>   As a first step, complete the CBT formulation activity below. At this stage, these will be hypotheses.
>
> - What are Mary's core beliefs about herself?
> - What are Mary's core belief about others?
> - What are her intermediate beliefs (assumptions and/or rules)?

I have completed this exercise. My conclusions at this point are tentative and are based on what we know so far about Mary. You will be able to compare your formulation to mine.

I propose that Mary had core beliefs of being *unlovable/unwanted* and also of being *dependent on others*. Mary's responses in the session were triggered by Patrick reminding her of the up-coming break in sessions. Mary's emotional reactions in the session are associated with Mary's core beliefs of others as being *rejecting* and *dismissive*, and *her expectations of being alone* for the rest of her life. She also appears to have intermediate beliefs around the importance of finding a partner and having a child – *If I have a family of my own, I will not be alone* (assumption). Given that she is nearing 40, she has a sense of urgency to find a partner. Her negative assumption may be – *If I don't have a partner/ child, I will be alone forever*.

In relation to the five-part model, the triggering event was Patrick reminding her that he was going away. Mary responds in an emotionally distressed way to this and begins to talk (behaviour) about how desperate she feels to have her own family.

Patrick's emotions in therapy

We can now reflect on Patrick's emotional reactions to Mary. We know less about Patrick's core and intermediate beliefs about self and others but we have enough information to be able to engage in some initial reflections.

When Mary showed distress about Patrick going away for two weeks and started talking in what seemed to be a 'desperate' way, Patrick experienced Mary as needy and as clinging to him emotionally. He is also likely to have had NATs in regard to her neediness and clinging. This reaction of Patrick's appeared to have been realistic, at least in part – as Mary herself appeared to be distressed about his time away indicating her own sense of neediness of her sessions with Patrick. We can propose then that this reaction of Patrick's was, at least in part, a normative reaction.

However, when Mary responded in this way, Patrick felt as if he wanted to push her away and also had thoughts about his mother and her neediness during childhood. This suggests a personal aspect to Patrick's emotional reactions at this point in time. This might have been quite a challenging situation for Patrick because it provoked negative automatic thoughts about needy women. It may also have provoked an intermediate belief that he cannot cope with needy women, and that he should avoid needy women.

This activation of personal beliefs and NATs creates an extra challenge for Patrick. He will need to reflect on how his negative beliefs and reactions to neediness in others have contributed to his emotional reaction and his urge to push the client away. He can also consider his emotional reactions as partly normative, as Mary's distress and behaviour has placed him in a challenging situation in regard to his time away. Many therapists would find this at least somewhat challenging.

Summary

This chapter aimed to deepen understanding of the four-step approach and especially the second and third steps that focus on understanding or conceptualising the client's (and therapist's) templates for relationships (self–other representations, core beliefs), and the interpersonal processes, including transference and countertransference, that arise in therapy sessions. In this chapter, we applied the approach to a new case study and reflected on this case from two perspectives – a psychodynamic perspective and a CBT perspective. The psychodynamic perspective examined the client and therapist transference and countertransference reactions while the cognitive-behavioural perspective examined the client and therapist emotional reactions in therapy to each other, using cognitive-behavioural concepts. In the final part of the chapter, we briefly considered the events in Mary and Patrick's therapeutic relationship (Chapter 3) from a CBT perspective.

While this chapter focused on understanding or conceptualising transference and countertransference reactions, the next chapter moves on to more active strategies for working through any disruptions that occur in the therapeutic relationship and alliance.

Recommended readings

Beck, J. (2011). *Cognitive Behavior Therapy: Basics and beyond*. New York, NY: Guilford Press.

Cartwright, C. & Read, J. (2011). An exploratory investigation of psychologists' responses to a method for considering 'objective' countertransference. *New Zealand Journal of Psychology, 40*, 46–54.

Cartwright, C., Rhodes, P., King, R., & Shires, A. (2015). A pilot study of a method for teaching clinical psychology trainees to conceptualise and manage countertransference. *Australian Psychologist, 50*, 148–156.

Cartwright, C., Barber, C., Cowie, S., & Thompson, N. (2018). A trans-theoretical training designed to promote understanding and management of countertransference for trainee therapists. *Psychotherapy Research, 28*, 517–532.

Cartwright, C., Cowie, S., Bavin, L. M., & Bennett Levy, J. (2019). Therapists' experiences of spontaneous mental imagery in therapy. *Clinical Psychologist, 23*, 225–236.

5

Countertransference and Therapeutic Ruptures

This chapter focuses on understanding and working therapeutically with disruptions to the therapeutic relationship and the therapeutic alliance. Disruptions to the alliance are also commonly referred to as 'alliance ruptures' in clinical writing and research. Transference and countertransference reactions often underlie or contribute to disruptions in the therapeutic alliance during the course of therapy. Countertransference reactions of the therapist also alert the therapist to potential disruptions in the therapeutic alliance from the client's perspective and, as discussed previously, can provide insight into what is happening for the client.

The impact of disruptions varies depending on the severity of the issues that arise between therapist and client. Some disruptions can be relatively minor and more easily repaired or resolved. Other disruptions may involve a significant rupture or breach in the therapeutic alliance and threaten the viability of therapy. A series of unresolved disruptions could lead to an alliance rupture. This chapter explores ways in which therapists can work with and repair disruptions or ruptures to the therapeutic alliance. We will consider the therapy events (including therapist and client attitudes and behaviours) that trigger disruptions, signs that a disruption has occurred, and the role of transference and countertransference. I will then introduce a process that therapists can use to resolve and repair disruptions to the therapeutic alliance. This is an approach that I developed over a number of years in my own work with clients. I also teach this to trainees who appear to find it helpful in their work with clients. The approach is likely be similar to practices that therapists use when working with disruptions and shares common elements with other approaches to alliance ruptures (e.g., Okamoto & Kazantzis, 2021; Safran, Muran, & Eubanks-Carter, 2011).

Disruptions to the therapeutic alliance

As discussed in Chapter 3, the therapeutic alliance is characterised by an affective bond and a collaborative working relationship between therapist and client. The collaborative relationship includes an understanding and agreement on the nature of the client's problem/s for which they sought help and the activities that are being undertaken to assist with these problems. The importance of the therapeutic alliance has been established in psychotherapy outcome research. Client ratings of the alliance are predictive of therapy outcomes (Horvarth et al., 2011; Flückiger et al., 2018). Disruptions to the alliance (or alliance ruptures) manifest as tensions or breakdowns in the relationship between therapist and client and these can lead to negative therapy outcomes, including clients disengaging from therapy (Safran et al., 2011).

Transference, countertransference, and the therapeutic alliance

The quality of the therapeutic alliance is likely to be influenced by both client and therapist factors as well as contextual factors related to the sociocultural circumstances of client, therapist, and treatment. Evidence for the impact of client factors can be seen in the variability of client outcomes, where some clients experience significant improvement in just a few sessions while others, including those with personality disorders, require much longer (Bohart & Tallman, 2010). An individual client's ability to form a therapeutic alliance is affected, in part, by the self–other representations held and the coping strategies or defences the client uses to manage emotional reactions to others. As discussed in Chapter 2, the development of self–other representations occurs not only within the family but also within the wider sociocultural context and this provides a backdrop to the transference reactions that clients may have towards their therapists that then influence the quality of the therapeutic alliance.

Therapist factors and therapist countertransference are influenced in part by the client's transference reactions and the way that clients relate to the therapist (objective countertransference). Countertransference is also influenced by therapists' personal issues and sensitivities (subjective countertransference) and the self–other representations and coping strategies that underlie their responses to clients.

Transference and countertransference reactions often contribute to or underlie disruptions to the therapeutic alliance. Being able to resolve these disruptions is important for clients, therapists, and therapeutic progress. Therapists are generally concerned when they sense or clearly experience evidence of clients experiencing alliance disruptions and recognise the importance of talking through and resolving problems that are impacting on the emotional bond and the collaborative relationship. However, there is now a body of research that supports these therapists' concerns. This research suggests that repairing disruptions to the alliance can have benefits for therapeutic relationships and outcomes (Safran et al., 2011). This chapter presents strategies that can assist therapists in repairing disruptions.

What causes disruptions?

We have talked previously about clients who may struggle to form a therapeutic alliance. In this section, we will reflect on the types of therapy events and therapist behaviours that can trigger disruptions. There are likely to be a myriad of possible triggers for clients that can lead them to feel tension or begin to doubt the therapy and/or the therapist. Some of these will involve therapist mistakes or therapist behaviours that are untherapeutic. We all engage in these sometimes, despite our attempts not to do so, because we are human. These may include:

• forgetting or being late for appointments
• misunderstanding a client, especially in regard to a sensitive issue
• making remarks or comments that are experienced as insensitive or unempathetic
• expressing countertransference reactions (such as frustration or annoyance) in an uncontained or unprocessed way, or allowing these to show in non-verbal reactions
• being critical of a client
• being tired or distracted or seeming uninterested

As you will see when you look at the list of the above responses, many of these therapist behaviours or responses may actually be linked to countertransference; for example, forgetting an appointment with a client could reflect some unconscious or conscious ambivalence about the client. On the other hand, it could simply reflect that therapists are stretching themselves too far and suggest that they need to engage in some more self-care and perhaps take things a little easier. Either way, it is likely to negatively impact – at least to some degree – on the client's feelings about the therapist.

Therapists may also engage in activities that we may consider therapeutic but are still triggering for clients. These include:

• encouraging a client to engage in activities that they do not want to do or find too challenging or distressing
• making an interpretation of a client's reaction that the client dislikes or feels is invalidating or insulting

Sometimes our mannerisms or the way we dress or behave remind a client of someone they know or have known and trigger a transference reaction that is uncomfortable. As we have discussed, different sociocultural backgrounds of client and therapist can also be triggering. You may recall Genia, a young woman of Afro-Caribbean descent (p. 28), who felt uncomfortable with her therapist's apparent wealth and 'upper crust' status.

Signs or signals from the client of a disruption

Clients will usually give some signs or signals that not all is well in the relationship between the two of you. As we have discussed throughout the book, it is really important to be attuned to clients and to monitor our interactions with them. In terms of the alliance, it is important to be aware of any changes in clients' non-verbal behaviours, their attitudes towards us, and their ways of relating to us. At any given moment in therapy, it is helpful to be attuned to the client and how they are feeling and reacting to what you have just said or done, and to be aware of any tension that might be arising between you. Thinking in terms of the therapeutic alliance we can consider:

- Is the client on board with me?
- Is the client working with me on the goals we established together?
- Is the client engaging with me in the tasks of therapy?
- Am I on board with and working with the client?

There will usually be some signs or signals from clients when problems are arising in the therapeutic alliance. These can vary from obvious client reactions, such as strong expressions of disagreement or hostility, through to more subtle changes in clients. Safran and Muran (2000) have pointed out that alliance ruptures can take the form of withdrawal or confrontation ruptures. Signs of withdrawal ruptures are likely to be more subtle and therefore go unnoticed by therapists, at least in the early stages of a disruption.

Clients themselves may or may not be cognisant of what is happening for them. They may be feeling uncomfortable and not understand why. They may be having negative thoughts about you and/or about other people generally or they may be feeling as if something is wrong in therapy and think that they are the problem. The intervention or activity that you are doing in therapy may be triggering for them and this may be affecting how they feel towards you. You will recall Eddie's experience when his therapist persisted in asking him about his childhood. Angeline did this for therapeutic reasons and it led to positive outcomes for Eddie but at the time it triggered a negative transference reaction in Eddie. His transference to others (and an other-representation) as abusive was triggered and he became angry and withdrawn towards his therapist, Angeline. Their therapeutic alliance was disrupted at these times although Angeline managed this disruption by persisting gently and giving Eddie her rationale for doing so.

It is also important to remember that clients' internal reactions may or may not be clearly reflected in their responses to therapists. Compliant clients, for example, may continue to try to look as if they are on board with us when, in reality, they are beginning to think that therapy is not working for them or that the therapist might become angry or annoyed with them if they do not do what they think is expected of them.

Over the years, I have observed and heard supervisees and trainees talk about a number of signs or signals from clients that a disruption has occurred or is occurring in the alliance. In the section below, I discuss some of the common signs you might observe in clients who are struggling to feel good towards their therapists and their therapeutic work.

Missing, cancelling or being late for appointments

When clients miss, cancel, or are late for appointments, it is important to consider that these could be signs that something is amiss in terms of their feelings about themselves, their therapy, and their therapists. Sometimes there will be practical reasons for clients missing an appointment or being late. Other times, this will reflect clients' ambivalence or doubts about therapy. If clients do not attend sessions or are late on a semi-regular basis, and there are no genuine practical reasons for this, then it most likely represents some ambivalence about therapy.

Clients behaving differently

Sometimes clients begin to behave differently although the changes can be quite subtle and you may doubt your perceptions. For example, a client may have been relating well to the therapist and talking quite openly about what was happening for them and what they were experiencing. However, the client may become quieter or the therapist may have a sense of the client withdrawing. Supervisees have described having a sense that 'a wall has gone up' or 'come down' between themselves and clients. This is often a sign that something is happening for the client that is impacting on the therapeutic alliance.

In order to reflect on this some more, we will go back to the case of Ana and think about the differences that the therapist observed in Ana between the first and second sessions, following the therapist cancelling her appointment due to illness. We will also follow the case of Ana through the next sections of the chapter as we consider different aspects of disruptions to the therapeutic alliance.

CASE STUDY: ANA'S STORY

We can reflect back on the experiences of Ana whose story we considered earlier (p. 39–40). Ana experienced a yearning as a child for someone, a woman, who would care for and look after her. She often experienced a sense of emptiness in her childhood and adult life and this led her to seek therapy. Ana really warmed to the therapist, Joan, when she met her for her first session and was excited about continuing therapy with her. Ana experienced the therapist as warm and kind. However, Joan cancelled the second session as she was sick and Ana went from 'feeling elated' to feeling as if she was crashing into an empty hole. The positive feelings about having found this therapist were gone. Ana was up and down for the week and became nervous before her next session with the therapist. She thought of cancelling but her good sense told her not to.

This therapy event, the cancelling of the client's appointment, had a marked effect on Ana – at least, for the time being. By the next session, Ana's demeanour had changed. Joan noticed this as soon as Ana entered her office. Ana seemed nervous and a little withdrawn and the therapist became concerned for Ana who seemed 'quite low'.

Pause and reflect: Cancelling a client's session

1. What signs do you notice in Ana that the beginning of the therapeutic alliance has been disrupted?
2. Have you ever had to cancel a session with a client? Did this lead to any change in the client's attitude towards you in the next session? What did you notice?
3. Have you ever had a therapist cancel a session, and, if so, how did that affect you?

We will return to this discussion again throughout the next sections of the chapter.

Getting better quickly

Clients can also talk about ending sessions because they are feeling better. This is not always a sign of a therapeutic disruption – there may be practical reasons for ending therapy or the clients may have genuinely made good progress and feel ready to end. However, sometimes this seems premature or out of the blue and the therapist's reaction may be one of surprise or some confusion, as this was unexpected. Therapists sometimes refer to these unexpected client reactions as a flight into health. Such a 'flight' can be understood as clients wishing to avoid difficulties that might be arising in the therapeutic relationship or because they are wanting to avoid the next stage of therapy, which might be confronting or threatening to them. They may also be having transference reactions to the therapist that lead them to want to end therapy.

At times, I have also had the impression that clients who prematurely (from my perspective) suggest that they are ready to end sessions may in fact be releasing me from what they perceive as the burden of themselves and their problems. When this has occurred and I have encouraged them to continue on, they have seemed relieved. This then appeared to confirm for me that the client wanted some reassurance that I really wished to continue on this difficulty journey with them.

Before moving on to the next sign of a disruption, we will reflect on a therapeutic situation that is relevant to the next topic.

Pause and reflect: Finding the therapist's absence difficult

Brendon had been seeing his therapist for six months and was really valuing his weekly sessions. He found that it helped him cope with his anxiety and his problems with his boss at work. His therapist Jethro took a three-week holiday. This was planned and Brendon knew about it well in advance. He thought it was really reasonable that Jethro take a holiday although he did find it quite difficult not seeing Jethro as he was used to doing.

During their first session back together, Brendon seemed to be relating to Jethro as he usually did. However, Jethro was surprised that Brendon appeared to have had difficulty with his best friend while Jethro was away. Brendon's friend was one of his greatest supports and was a fairly easy-going person from what Jethro had come to understand. Now, for the first time, Brendon was going through a litany of complaints about his friend. His friend was not able to go out to the movies with him one evening, his friend was annoying when they played tennis together, and his friend didn't really seem to understand how anxious Brendon was feeling.

This seemed odd to Jethro – it was so out of the blue.

1. Have you experienced something like this with a client, and what did you think was happening at the time?
2. What do you think might be happening here with Brendon?
3. What might you ask or say to Brendon if you were Jethro, and what is your rationale for this?

Other people are hurting the client or making the client angry

Sometimes clients may find it difficult to manage their thoughts and feelings towards therapists. They may want to express some negative thoughts and feelings but not know how to do this or feel safe enough to do it, or alternatively, they may have negative reactions to the therapist but not really understand that it is an option for them to discuss these reactions. Sometimes then clients may begin to talk more about how hurt they are by others who have been insensitive or uncaring, or their feelings of anger towards others who have hurt, rejected, disappointed, or wounded them in some way. Sometimes this will be what the client needs to talk about. Sometimes clients may be displacing their feelings towards the therapist onto other/s in their daily lives. Talking about feelings towards another person may also be as close as clients can get towards telling therapists how they feel towards them and their responses or interventions. Hence, it is important to be alert to the content of clients' talk about others – especially if this changes in some way.

Negative comments or actions towards the therapist

Clients can give clear signals that they are upset with or have negative feelings towards the therapist. This could include making comments like, 'If you say so', 'I think I should know how I feel!', 'You don't really understand' or 'You don't know how hard it is'. It can also include non-verbal responses – shrugs of the shoulder, avoiding eye contact, raising eyebrows, or raising or lowering the voice. Sometimes clients will also make negative comments about therapy interventions, 'This doesn't seem to be getting us anywhere', 'I can't see how this will help', 'I've tried this before and it doesn't work' or 'I can't understand where this is going'.

Clients can also make negative comments about us and this can be challenging especially for trainees and beginning therapists. Some clients – perhaps those with issues around dominance – will question young therapists' experience, 'How long have you been working as a therapist?', 'When did you begin your training?', or observations like, 'You're about the same age as my daughter'. All of the above are fairly clear signals to the therapist that there is a disruption to the alliance or that there are difficulties in establishing the alliance.

Direct expressions of criticism or anger

Sometimes clients will directly criticise or express anger at therapists. Sometimes criticism or anger may be warranted – that is, the client has a right to feel this way. All therapists sometimes make mistakes, misunderstand situations, and take actions that upset clients. Sometimes the strength of the criticisms or anger will reflect clients' struggles with emotion regulation and difficulty expressing themselves assertively rather than aggressively. This form of client expression is also a clear signal to the therapist that there are issues with the therapeutic alliance.

In the section above, we have considered some of the common signs and/or signals that we as therapists receive from clients that alert us to problems within the therapeutic alliance.

Pause and reflect: Signs of a therapeutic disruption

We have considered a number of signs that the client is experiencing a therapeutic disruption/rupture. These are summarised below:

- Missing, cancelling or being late for appointments
- Behaving differently from usual
- Getting better quickly
- Others are hurting or making the client angry
- Negative comments or actions
- Direct expression of criticism or anger

    1. Have you experienced any of the above recently? How did this emerge?
    2. Are there other client signs or signals that you have noticed that I have not included above?

Therapists' early warning signs

Throughout the book, we have explored the importance of monitoring our own reactions to clients. Our reactions to clients, including our countertransference reactions, are often a source of information for us and will help us to reflect on what might be happening for the client at any moment in therapy. They also alert us to the need to contain and manage our emotions in a way that is helpful for the client and therapy processes. The previous section addressed the importance of being aware of and monitoring clients' reactions within therapy. Our own countertransference reactions and our senses and intuitions will also alert us to any problems that may be emerging in the therapeutic alliance.

Sometimes we are barely conscious of our own subtle reactions. Our countertransference reactions to clients can manifest as bodily experiences. We may begin to feel physically uncomfortable, experience twinges, feel our neck or another part of our body becoming stiff, or feel a tightness in the chest. We may feel a bit bored or sleepy. We may feel sad out of the blue or notice the stirrings of irritation or anger. We may feel frightened or anxious. We may have a sense of dread. We may simply have a sense that something is amiss or something is not right or that we are losing connection with the client. We may have a sense that the client has become distant or that the client is going to end sessions prematurely.

Putting together the signs

Therapists might not use the terms disruption or rupture as they reflect on these types of events within therapy. Therapists may be more likely to think,

'Something is not going well here. What should I do about it? Is now the right time to bring this up with the client or should I wait and see what happens next? Maybe this will pass'.

At times though it becomes clear that the client and therapist are not working well together. There is disruption to the goals, tasks, and/or therapy bond that make up the therapeutic alliance. A sense of this disruption may have been present for a while, the sense may have arisen in the current session, or it may feel like it has come to a head.

Therapists can ask themselves:

- Has something occurred between us or in the therapeutic context that is difficult for the client and impacting on the alliance?
- What signs, if any, have I noticed in the client's behaviour?
- What am I experiencing – do I also have a sense that the client is not working with me or that the bond with the client is weakened?

The next section will introduce therapeutic strategies for exploring and, if possible, repairing the therapeutic disruption.

Working with disruptions to the therapeutic alliance

Disruptions are common in therapy – sometimes they are minor and easily resolved as they arise and sometimes ruptures may be so serious that they threaten the viability of the therapy. Working through the disruption involves talking with the client about what has been happening for the client in therapy, including how they have been feeling towards the therapist and therapy, developing a common understanding, and negotiating any changes or adjustments that might be needed. Below, I present a series of stages that represent a process of working through disruptions with clients. Therapeutic situations vary and the processes of talking through disruptions can evolve differently each time. Some of the stages outlined below may not be necessary or therapists may proceed in a somewhat different order. Nevertheless, it is useful to be aware of the processes that are helpful and the order in which these might emerge.

Reflecting on the client's experiences of therapy event/s

Initially, and if time allows, it is helpful to spend some time reflecting on the therapeutic disruption before attempting to work through it with the client. You can consider what was happening prior to noticing any signs in yourself or the client that all was not well in the alliance. It is also helpful to develop some realistic hypotheses about the client's experience. To illustrate this process, let's consider the reflections that Ana's therapist engaged in *prior to* her second session with Ana, and following the cancellation of Ana's previous appointment.

Ana's therapist, Joan, was concerned about cancelling her clients' appointments the previous week. She had to do this, however, as she was very unwell. Joan was particularly concerned about the impact on Ana, given that they had only had one session together. At least with her other clients, she had more established relationships. Ana had also talked in the first session about her mother's illness when she was a child and how alone she felt and still feels at times. Ana had also seemed to really warm to Joan and be excited at beginning therapy. She thought it was possible that Ana might have found it quite distressing when the receptionist rang to cancel. Hence, Joan observed Ana as she entered the room and they began to talk. She noticed quite a dramatic change in Ana from the previous fortnight. Ana spoke very quietly, seemed nervous, and avoided eye contact with Joan. Joan's thoughts that Ana would have found this time difficult were confirmed. Joan had thought about what she would do if this were the case.

In this case, Joan was aware that Ana might find the cancellation difficult. She took the opportunity to reflect on this ahead of seeing Ana again. During this reflection process, she imagined what the experience would have been like for Ana. She reflected on the theme of emotional abandonment in Ana's life and her tentative formulation that Ana holds a self-representation of herself as abandoned/left alone in relation to the other who is abandoning. Based on this initial tentative formulation, Joan had prepared herself for signs of a disruption to the very early development of a therapeutic alliance with Ana.

Beginning a discussion about the therapy event/s

Therapists sometimes hope for the best and carry on with the therapy session/s, even when they have noticed that the client is not really on board with them. Conflict is difficult for therapists just as it is for people generally and some therapists might find conflict even more difficult because of their own history, the beliefs they have about conflict, and the emotions it triggers. Preparing to talk to the client about problems that have emerged will help build confidence and also make it more likely that the conversation with the client will go well. This could begin with a simple query or question: 'I'm wondering how things are going for you in therapy at the moment?'.

This could be enough to start a conversation – the client might give some indication about their feelings and a conversation about whatever is happening could begin. Sometimes, or perhaps even often, a client might initially deny that there is a problem. The client, for example, might say, 'Everything is fine!'. If this happens, it can be helpful to let the client know that you have observed something about them. This has to be worded carefully as clients can feel embarrassed or ashamed about having negative thoughts and feelings.

They may also be feeling distrustful towards the therapist and so wording is important. The therapist could respond in this way:

> *Therapist*: I might be wrong about this but I have the feeling that you are a little unhappy or unsure about how we are going in therapy at the moment? Is something happening for you that you could tell me about?

At times, it might be more useful to name the behaviour or change in behaviour that you have observed in the client.

> *Therapist*: I think I've noticed – tell me if I am wrong – that you do not seem to be quite as involved in therapy as you were before. I've noticed in the last two sessions that you look down at the floor quite a lot and sometimes you seem unhappy or unsure about something, perhaps what we are talking about? You seem a little different to me?

It can be useful to use tentative language, as above, so that you convey interest in the client's opinion and demonstrate that you understand that you do not necessarily know what is happening for them and you are concerned about how the client is feeling. In this way, you are not pronouncing on the client's experience but rather adopting a naïve inquirer position.

At this point, we will reflect further on the experiences of Ana and Joan.

Pause and reflect: Being Ana's therapist

Let's reflect on the experiences of Ana and Joan. Ana was at a very early stage of building a therapeutic alliance with her therapist Joan when Joan cancelled her appointment. You have read how difficult this was for Ana and her thoughts and feelings following the cancellation. She has come to her second session looking nervous, withdrawn, and down.
   If you were Joan, how would you lead into this with Ana?

- What would you want to convey to Ana through both your words and your non-verbal behaviour?
- What would you say to Ana – what actual words would you use?
- How do you think Ana might react?
- If she said that there was no problem, how would you respond to that?
- Finally, were you hesitant about raising this issue with Ana and, if so, what were your concerns?

It is also important to note that sometimes if a client insists that there is no problem – as long as you have given them the opportunity to open up about this – then it is best to let it go at that time. We can think of this as the client not feeling able or ready to talk about what is happening between them and the therapist. Ana, for example, may have felt shame at times in her life due to her sense of neediness. She may have felt bad about having felt so good about the therapist and about being so excited to see her again. She may also feel bad for having been so affected by the cancellation. She may not be able to talk about this yet.

Normalising the client's experiences of the event/s

It can be useful to normalise clients' experiences and reactions if they are having difficulty talking about their experience of the events in therapy. The process of normalising includes talking in general terms about aspects of therapy or therapist behaviours that clients can find challenging. This can assist clients to talk more openly about their experiences with you in therapy. This can be particularly helpful if a client is feeling embarrassed or ashamed about their emotional responses. Joan's conversation below with Ana illustrates the potential value of normalising therapy experiences for clients.

Joan: Ana, I'm wondering how you are feeling today. You seem a little worried or perhaps tired?

Ana: I'm OK thank you. I am just a little tired. It's been a bit of a stressful week at work.

Joan: Would you like to talk about that today?

Ana: No, it's OK. It's just a busy period.

Joan: Yes, I remember you said that you had a busy period coming up. I did think about that when I was unwell and had to cancel our appointment. I was a bit concerned that it would be hard for you – my cancelling.

Ana: I fully understand that – that's what people need to do when they are sick.

Joan: Yes, I think so too. [Pause] On the other hand, though, I did wonder how it would be for you as we had only had one session together and it might have felt quite sudden to have that happen?

Ana: Perhaps. I hadn't thought about that.

Joan: It is quite normal and common for clients to feel a little upset or anxious if a therapist cancels out of the blue. It would be normal if it was a bit difficult for you.

[You will note here that Joan is also doing a little minimising in using the phrase 'a little upset or anxious'. This is to support Ana to begin to feel OK about talking about how she felt. If Joan said, 'It would be normal if you were really distressed by this' it could be confusing for the client and also a bit frightening]

Ana: Perhaps it was a bit hard, I guess. I'm not sure.

In the conversation above, Joan has gently persisted with the idea that it can be stressful for clients when therapists cancel and it may have affected Ana.

Exploring and understanding the client's experience of the event/s

The main goal of this stage of the process is to come to understand the client's subjective experiences of the event (or therapy intervention) that has been difficult for them and is impacting on the therapeutic alliance. What has the client been feeling? What are their thoughts? How are they thinking and feeling about the therapist, the therapy, and themselves in therapy?

Once the client gives some indication – as Ana has – that there is or has been something difficult for them, then the therapist can support the client to talk about this some more. Below is an illustration of Joan's approach to exploring the event and its impact on Ana along with the impact this is now having on Ana's response to her therapist.

Joan: Can you tell me what it was like when you got the telephone call cancelling the appointment, Ana?

Ana: I was just surprised, it was a bit of a shock, I wasn't expecting it so … [voice drifts off, and Ana looks down]

Joan: Yes, it must have come out of the blue for you. I'm wondering if it has affected how you are feeling about beginning therapy? Did you have any thoughts about that?

Ana: [Laughs slightly and nervously smiles at the therapist] I suppose I thought that therapy is meant to make you feel better, not worse.

Joan: [Nods and pauses] Did you have any other thoughts about my cancelling that were a bit difficult for you? [Pause. Ana is quiet] I would like to understand how it was for you.

Ana: I guess I wondered if you were sick of me already. [Ana looks sad]

Joan: [At this point, Joan thinks about Ana's mother's illness and wonders if Ana felt as a child that she had somehow made her mother sick or that her mother was in hospital because she was sick of Ana. Joan decides not to bring this up at this stage as it is still early days in therapy. This will be something to think about later and is useful for her formulation of Ana's problems and her self–other representations] So you thought maybe I was sick of you and perhaps didn't want to see you that day?

Ana: [Ana is looking more animated and seems more engaged] Sort of.

Joan: It must have been a bit awful to think and feel like that.

Ana: I guess so. Although I sort of knew it was unlikely but it did throw me a bit. I was a bit anxious coming today.

Joan: I'm wondering if my cancelling led you to feel a bit unsure about therapy and maybe about me. After all, we haven't really gotten to know each other yet so you wouldn't know if this was a common or rare thing.

Ana: I think I was just deflated. I was really looking forward to talking again so I took it a bit hard. I think I over-reacted.

Joan: I think it's understandable Ana that it was difficult for you, especially given that we had only just met. And it wasn't good timing for you. It makes it harder for you, I think.

Ana: Yes, it was quite hard.

If Joan and Ana had a more established therapeutic relationship with a strong therapeutic alliance, Joan could attempt to take this deeper. However, she notices that Ana is perking up. She has perhaps appreciated Joan's interest and concern, and she has managed to express that it was difficult for her and it did affect her week and how she felt about coming to the session. She has also shared something quite personal – her thought that Joan might have become sick of her. Joan decides to move on to the next stage of attempting to further repair the relationship with Ana.

Acknowledging and validating the client's experiences

The overall aim of this process is to acknowledge and validate the client's experience of the event/s that led to the disruption. In the previous stage, the therapist has helped the client to talk about their thoughts and feelings about the event that occurred or the therapy as it was progressing. However, this is not necessarily resolved. Some further discussions or actions may be needed now.

One of the questions which sometimes arises is whether the therapist should apologise to the client if the therapist does something that upsets the client. In Joan's case, she was sick. It was important that she did not come to work and that she took time to recover. However, Joan could express her concern for how the cancellation impacted on Ana.

Joan: Ana, it couldn't be helped. I felt that I needed to cancel my appointments last week. But I really do regret that this happened as it did and that it was such poor timing for you.

Ana: That's OK. It's not your fault. These things happen.

Joan: I really do understand how you felt. I think many clients would also have found this difficult and perhaps had doubts about me.

Thank you for telling me how you felt. And I'm really glad we talked about this.

Ana: So am I.

In some situations, the therapist has made a mistake and triggered the client's reaction, which has led to the disruption. Often these may represent therapists' failures in empathic attunement and countertransference behaviours towards clients. Ana's therapist, Joan, did not make a mistake. In order to explore how a therapist can take responsibility if they do make a mistake, we will consider the case of Joanne and her therapist.

Taking responsibility if appropriate

Sometimes a therapist has made a mistake, which has triggered the client's reaction and led to the disruption. We have talked about the types of mistakes that therapists can make that understandably lead to negative client reactions. Disruptions also occur because of therapists' lack of empathic understanding for the client and countertransference behaviours.

Joanne had seen her therapist, Meena, for ten sessions when the disruption occurred. She was seeing the therapist for assistance with her depression, which was triggered when her partner left her for another woman. Joanne had a tendency during sessions to begin to chastise herself for being responsible for the end of her relationship. At other times, she was very blaming towards her ex-partner Andre and Andre's new partner.

Her therapist Meena became aware that something had been amiss over the last two sessions. When she thought about it, she decided that the disruption appeared to have occurred towards the end of the last session when Joanne had been talking about Andre's faults in quite a condemning way. Something happened around that time as Joanne showed signs of irritation and seemed to shut down. Joanne's change in attitude continued into the current session. As noted above, Meena became aware that something was amiss over these two sessions. She asked Joanne how she was feeling about therapy and when Joanne said, 'Fine', she decided it was important to explore further, as something was clearly bothering the client. She was also a little bit worried that Joanne might get up and leave the session.

Meena: Joanne, I think I've noticed – tell me if I am wrong – that you do not seem to be quite as involved in therapy as you were before. I've noticed in the last few minutes of last week and today that you seem unhappy or unsure about something, perhaps what we are talking about? Or I'm wondering if there is something I have done that is bothering you?

Joanne: Maybe.

Meena: Can you tell me what it was? I would really like to understand.

Joanne: I thought therapists were supposed to support their clients.

Meena: I think so too. Do you feel that I am not supporting you?

Joanne: You said last week that I am better off without Andre.

Meena: Oh. [Pause] Yes, I did say that – I remember saying that you might be better off without him. Was that upsetting for you – my saying that?

Joanne: Do you really think I am better off without him!! After everything I have told you about how important he was to me? I don't feel better off without him. [Joanne is raising her voice and looking angrily at Meena]

At this point, Meena reflects on what she was feeling when she made that comment. She realises now that she felt tired of hearing about Andre's faults while at the same time hearing about Joanne's desire to reunite with him. There was also something about how Joanne was talking too that irritated her – a sense that she was whining. Then as she thought this, she remembered that Joanne had always been told that she was 'whining' as a child when she tried to express her feelings. She wondered if she had taken on a critical Parent position in relation to Joanne's distressed Child. She thinks she will need to reflect on this after the session. Now she needs to respond to Joanne. She does this initially by putting herself in her position and reflecting on how that statement might have felt. She validates Joanne's feelings.

Meena: Yes, I see what you mean Joanne. You are here because it has been so difficult for you losing Andre. I think I was reacting to some of the stories you have told me about how difficult he could be at times. But yes, I can see that that could have been quite hurtful for you. [Pause] What did you feel when I said that?

Joanne: Hurt and annoyed. It felt a bit like a put-down or like you were telling me to shut up. And then I just withdrew. I've had enough of people treating me like that in my life.

Meena realises that Joanne did accurately pick up the irritation in her voice and that she was wanting Joanne to stop. However, she also needs to unpack this more. She is aware of the problems of sharing countertransference feelings especially when both therapist and client are emotionally aroused and she has not had time to process this. At the moment, she is going to validate Joanne and somehow also leave this conversation open for the future.

Meena: That's fair enough, Joanne. I understand what you mean. And I'm really glad that you are telling me now how you felt. [Pause] I can see what I said was insensitive to you.

Joanne: [Long pause] It's not really your fault. A lot of my friends are getting sick of hearing about this, I think. [Joanne looks at Meena and gives a half-smile] Actually, I had a really bad experience with Andre this week – don't give me a lecture if I tell you about it!

Meena: [Smiles] Tell me about it then.

In the next chapter, we will come back to this therapeutic situation with Meena and Joanne. For the time being, the therapeutic alliance that she had built with Joanne over the last ten weeks may have helped cushion the effects of her countertransference reaction.

Thinking about future sessions

It can also be really helpful to think about what can be learnt from this experience and what this might mean for future sessions. Collaborating on future plans can also help to re-strengthen the therapeutic alliance, as in this example with Joan and Ana.

Joan: I'm wondering if there is something we can take away from this that we can use in our future sessions.

Ana: I'm not sure.

Joan: Well, I really liked that you told me how you had been thinking and feeling. I really appreciate you doing that.

Ana: Thank you.

Joan: I'm wondering if there is anything I could do in the future if another situation arose where I needed to cancel – although I must say I don't expect to do that and rarely have to cancel.

Ana: I'm not sure. [Long pause] I did find it hard getting the message from the receptionist. [Pause] I might prefer it if you texted me.

Joan: So hearing from me more directly might be helpful?

Ana: Yes, I think so. Also, next time if it happens again, I'll be better prepared. I think it was the shock of it this time.

Joan: OK. Let's do that. I am happy to text you if I did become unwell again.

Ana: Thank you. [Smiles]

Hence, Joan the therapist has made one suggestion – to keep an open channel between them. This suggests to Ana that they can talk about problems in therapy as they arise. Ana has also offered a suggestion – that it would be easier for her if Joan texted her if she had to cancel an appointment again. Joan feels OK about doing this and agrees to do so. Hence, they have worked together, increased their collaboration and hopefully enhanced the newly developing therapeutic alliance.

Linking back to the client's history of relationships

Sometimes when a therapeutic alliance has been built, the therapist may be able to link what has happened between the therapist and client to difficulties

Strategies for repairing disruptions or alliance ruptures

- Beginning a discussion of the therapy event/s
- Normalising the client's experiences of the event/s
- Exploring and understanding the client's experiences of the event/s
- Acknowledging and validating the client's experiences
- Taking responsibility if appropriate
- Thinking about future sessions

in previous relationships. For Ana, this would include the impact of her mother's hospitalisations on her. I have previously hypothesised that Ana developed a self–other representation of self as unwanted/abandoned and other as abandoning/rejecting. These representations and the associated emotions appear to have been triggered by Joan's cancellation of their second appointment. One of the common aims of most therapeutic approaches is to assist clients to become aware of and adjust problematic patterns of relating to others. As yet, Joan and Ana have not talked about Ana's intimate relationships and friendships with others. However, Ana is likely to have some sensitivity towards rejection and feeling unwanted in relationships and she may talk about this further as therapy proceeds. As this happens, it becomes possible for Joan to link what she experiences in other relationships with what she experiences in therapy with Joan. At this point in therapy, however, this would be premature.

Summary

This chapter has considered disruptions (also referred to as ruptures) to the therapeutic alliance that occur in therapy situations. These can range from relatively minor bumps on the road through to ruptures that threaten the viability of therapy. Transference and countertransference reactions often contribute to or underlie these disruptions. Being able to resolve these disruptions and repair the alliance are essential for the progress of therapy, and for management of countertransference.

We discussed some of the common causes of disruptions, including therapist behaviours based on countertransference reactions and challenging therapeutic interventions. It is important for therapists to monitor the therapeutic alliance and be aware of any signs or signals from clients that they are not on board with the therapist. Therapists are also advised to monitor their own reactions including their intuitions, senses, and countertransference feelings. We then examined a process for resolving disruptions, including a series of interventions in which the therapist encourages the client to talk openly about what is happening for them and then to address any issues that arise, to the satisfaction of both of them. The overall aim of this process is to repair and strengthen the therapeutic alliance so that both therapist and client are working well together on the tasks and goals of therapy to which they have agreed.

Recommended readings

Gelso, C. (2014). A tripartite model of the therapeutic relationship: Theory, research, and practice. *Psychotherapy Research, 24,* 117–131.

Katzow, A. W. & Safran, J. D. (2007). Recognizing and resolving ruptures in the therapeutic alliance. In P. Gilbert & R. L. Leahy (Eds.), *The therapeutic relationship in the cognitive behavioral psychotherapies* (pp. 90–105). New York: Routledge.

Okamoto, A. & Kazantzis, N. (2021). Alliance ruptures in cognitive behavioral therapy: A cognitive conceptualization. *Journal of Clinical Psychology, 77*(2), 384–397.

Safran, J. & Muran, J. C. (2000). *Negotiating the therapeutic alliance.* New York, NY: Guilford Press.

Safran, J. D., Muran, J. C., & Eubanks-Carter, C. (2011). Repairing alliance ruptures. *Psychotherapy, 48,* 80–87.

6

Managing Countertransference in Practice

Chapter 3 introduced the four-step approach to understanding and managing countertransference. Chapter 4 focused mainly on the second and third steps designed to assist with understanding or conceptualising transference and counter-transference reactions as they arise in therapy situations. Chapter 5 focused on recognising and repairing alliance disruptions or ruptures. Transference and countertransference reactions and behaviours often underlie and/or contribute to disruptions. This current chapter now returns to the fourth step – managing countertransference. Managing countertransference refers to managing coun-tertransference in such a way that negative impacts are minimised, and using the countertransference reaction, when this is possible, in a way that is helpful for therapy. Hence, this chapter examines a range of practices that may assist therapists with managing countertransference and discusses in some more depth the ideas introduced in Chapter 4.

The four steps

1. Monitoring and being aware of countertransference responses.
2. Reflecting on the client's patterns of relating to others.
3. Developing hypotheses about the interpersonal processes.
4. Managing the countertransference reactions.

These include strategies and practices that may enhance awareness, developing formulations of your clients' templates for relationships to assist in understanding countertransference, containing countertransference reactions and moving back into the Adult, and adopting an empathic view of the client. We will then consider how countertransference can be used as a tool in therapy and ways in which therapists can check out their hypotheses regarding clients' subjective experiences in sessions. The chapter then will move on to an area that constitutes particular challenges in regard to countertransference – sexual countertransference – and will end with a discussion of the pros and cons of sharing countertransference reactions with clients.

Awareness of countertransference

As discussed throughout the book, we need first to be aware of our countertransference reactions in order to manage them. All psychotherapeutic approaches emphasise the importance of therapist self-awareness. This includes therapists having insight into their responses within relationships in daily lives, and self-awareness during therapy sessions. Self-awareness in sessions refers to therapists' abilities to monitor and be aware of their reactions towards clients and the therapy situation – thoughts, feelings, bodily reactions, imagery, urges, behaviours – at any moment in time.

Developing awareness of how we respond in relationships in everyday life will also contribute to awareness of ourselves as we relate to clients. Both levels of self-awareness are vital components of any approach to understanding and managing countertransference.

Therapist self-awareness

Therapist personal insight – This involves being aware of or having insight into patterns of relating to others, including beliefs about self and other (for example, self–other representations or core beliefs) that underlie these relationship patterns, having insight into our sensitivities, needs, and motivations, and our coping strategies or defences. It is also important to be aware of any particular biases we have that may impact on our responses to clients.

Self-awareness in sessions – This means monitoring and being aware – at any moment in time – of reactions to clients or the therapy situation/context, including awareness of thoughts, feelings, bodily reactions, imagery, urges, and behaviours.

Therapist personal insight and awareness increases the likelihood that the therapist will be aware of countertransference reactions in therapy.

While it is vital that therapists maintain awareness of their responses to clients, it may be one of the most demanding tasks. For beginning therapists, this can be challenging as there is much to concentrate on, including what is happening for the client, goals for any given session, the overall therapy plan, dealing with any unexpected events that occur, and maintaining the therapeutic alliance. There is also some evidence that we may overestimate our expertise as we become more experienced; for example, research suggests that the therapeutic effectiveness of many experienced therapists declines somewhat over time, although some individuals maintain their levels of competency and are exceptions to this (Goldberg et al., 2016). It is worth keeping in mind then that as we gain more experience, there may be a tendency towards complacency or perhaps some fatigue that can lead us to be less attentive and questioning of our own reactions.

Developing self-awareness

Individual therapists vary in degrees of self-awareness. However, there are activities that therapists can engage in to increase self-awareness. Many therapists believe that they gained increased understanding of themselves and their reactions as a result of undertaking their own therapy. Attending to ourselves, the experiences that have shaped us, and our patterns of relating to others, in an intensive environment with input and feedback from a skilled therapist, is something that is likely to be valuable to many therapists. Some schools of psychotherapy and training programmes require trainees to engage in their own therapy. Others simply recommend it. By undertaking therapy or through their own process of self-discovery, therapists can increase awareness of themselves.

Earlier, I also recommended developing a formulation of the self–other representations and coping strategies that underlie our responses to others in everyday life. Readers can use these concepts or other concepts that make up the therapeutic approach/es that they use in their work with clients. Having a self-formulation assists us to make sense of our countertransference reactions as they occur.

Self-awareness and countertransference

Noah was 50 years old. It was his first session with a couple. The woman, Janet, was upset with her husband, Rob, whom she described as 'distant'. She said that he avoided spending time with her and was always reading or on the internet when they were at home. Janet cried as she talked about Rob's coldness towards her and also his bossiness when it came to household chores.

(Continued)

> Noah, the therapist, found himself getting irritated with Janet. He felt some dislike for her and how she was behaving in such a demanding way. Rob, on the other hand, seemed quite personable and Noah found himself feeling compassionate towards Rob and thinking that it is no wonder that Rob does not want to spend time with Janet. He felt like rescuing Rob from his very challenging wife.
>
> Importantly, Noah noticed these negative countertransference thoughts, feelings, and urges. He reminded himself that he found his own divorce 10 years ago – and his wife's tears and complaints at that time – almost unbearable. He recalled that he disliked his wife intensely at that time although these feelings did not last.
>
> What could have happened if Noah had not recognised his response as counter-transferential?

Reflective practice activities

There are activities that therapists can engage in that may enhance awareness of countertransference reactions. The first of these involves therapists making a commitment to regularly reflecting on their reactions to clients. Using the reflective practice guide provided at the end of Chapter 3 is one method that therapists can use. The guide leads therapists through the four steps that were completed in Chapters 3 and 4, and regular use of the guide is likely to increase awareness and conceptualisation of countertransference.

Another strategy that may be helpful relates to Jeffrey Hayes and Charles Gelso's (Hayes, 1995; Gelso & Hayes, 2007) five-component model of countertransference, which explores the origins, triggers, manifestations, effects, and management of countertransference reactions. In a recent study, Jeffrey Hayes, colleagues and I trialled this five-component model as a method of reflective practice for trainee psychologists (Cartwright, Hayes, Yang, & Shires, 2021). The model appeared to provide the trainees with a systematic method for thinking through their countertransference reactions.

You will find an illustration of this below. I have re-introduced the therapist and client from the previous chapter. Meena had been working with Joanne assisting her with her depression following the end of the relationship with her partner Andre. Joanne spoke repeatedly about Andre's faults after having talked about how she could not live without him. Meena felt as if Joanne was 'whining' and 'going around in circles'. She made the comment, 'Perhaps you are better off without him'. Following this, Joanne became withdrawn and Meena realised in the following session that they were experiencing an alliance rupture.

In the activity below, Meena used the five-component model to reflect on her reaction to Joanne in the previous session. Note that Meena was not fully conscious of her countertransference reaction and behaviour at the time, although she was able to recognise it once she focused on the interaction that had occurred.

Meena reflects on her countertransference reaction using the five-component model

Therapy situation

Joanne was talking about her ex's faults in a condemning way after she had been talking about her strong desire and need to get back with him. She had been doing this for several sessions despite my attempts to lead her in more productive directions. I felt she was doing this in a 'whiny' way.

Manifestations

I felt tired of hearing about her ex. In retrospect, I think I felt exasperated. I had a sense of going around in circles. I was really irritated by Joanne's whiny voice. I made the comment, 'Perhaps you are better off without him' which, in retrospect, was a manifestation of my irritation at Joanne and a countertransference behaviour.

Origins

I sometimes feel irritated with clients if I feel they are whining. There is something about the whining that gets to me. I felt Joanne was whining at me as if I had to do something to make it right. But I also had a sister who used to whine when she couldn't do what she wanted and she usually got her way. As a child, I felt that this was unfair. But this is different as Joanne has a history of not getting her way. I need to reflect on this more.

Effects

Joanne closed down or shut off. In the next session, it became clear that she had been hurt and angry and this was what led to her withdrawal.

Management

I didn't really manage this countertransference reaction in the moment. I wasn't aware of my emotions. I have talked this through now with Joanne and I think that I have repaired the rupture but I do need to reflect more on why I felt and acted like this, and also on the meaning of Joanne's 'whiny' behaviour, as this was a trigger for me.

Hence, the five-component model (Hayes, 1995; Gelso & Hayes, 2007) focuses the therapist on the different aspects of countertransference and leads to a process of reflection that is quite systematic. You may benefit from using this model yourself in your reflections on countertransference. Consider trialling the model to see if it helps to increase your awareness and also understanding of your reactions to clients.

Reflective practice: Developing awareness of my countertransference

You could use the Hayes' (1995) five-component model to reflect on your countertransference reactions. To do this, choose a countertransference reaction that you would like to understand better. Write about:

- What was happening in the session at the time of your countertransference reaction?
- How did your countertransference manifest (feelings, thoughts, bodily reactions, images, urges, behaviours)?
- What appeared to trigger your reaction?
- What might be the personal origins of your reaction?
- What were the effects of your reaction?
- How did you manage your reaction and how might you do this differently in the future?

You can then observe if completing this activity has any impact on your countertransference, and if it has any other benefits.

Mindfulness and meditation

Jon Kabat-Zinn is acknowledged as having introduced mindfulness meditation into Western therapeutic practices in the early 1990s. Kabat-Zinn is a professor of medicine who studied and practised meditation under Zen Buddhist teachers, and integrated his experience of meditation into the development of mindfulness-based stress reduction (MBSR) programmes for people struggling with pain and illness in their lives. These programmes and other developments related to mindfulness have proven successful in helping people with mental health problems and mindfulness training has now become a core component of a number of psychotherapy approaches including Dialectical Behaviour Therapy (DBT), Acceptance and Commitment Therapy (ACT), and Mindfulness-Based CBT. Trainees and therapists are often encouraged to train in mindfulness meditation themselves in order to enhance their own clinical practice and to be able to introduce mindfulness practices to clients.

Mindfulness

According to Jon Kabat-Zinn (2003), mindfulness is 'the awareness that emerges through paying attention on purpose, in the present moment, and non-judgmentally to the unfolding of experience moment to moment' (p. 145). Mindfulness refers to a state or quality of consciousness. The ability to respond mindfully in the moment is developed through the practices of mindfulness meditation. Mindfulness is:

- intentional
- experiential and focused directly on the present moment
- non-judgmental.

Mindfulness is intentional in its focus on the current reality as it is, experiential in its focus on the present moment experience, and non-judgmental in its focus on compassionate or 'heart' acceptance of things as they are, rather than things as they could or should be (Williams, Teasdale, Segal, & Kabat-Zinn, 2007).

As those of you who have experienced mindfulness training will know, mindfulness meditation directs attention to the present moment with a focus on the breath and breathing, and on bodily experiences and sensations. The attentional focus on experience in the here-and-now suspends judgments or interpretations of the experience. This develops the capacity to experience internal events, including very unpleasant or aversive emotional experiences, without pushing these away or being overcome by them. Hence, mindfulness practice can lead to increased acceptance of emotional experience rather than experiential avoidance.

THE BENEFITS OF MINDFULNESS MEDITATION FOR THERAPEUTIC WORK

As Kabat-Zinn (2021) wrote, mindfulness is of value as it takes up 'the challenge of relating wisely to any experience – whether it is pleasant, unpleasant, or neutral, wanted or unwanted, even horrific or unthinkable' (p. 1034). Some therapists and researchers suggest that the development of mindfulness qualities is likely to benefit therapists in their practices and may help therapists be aware of and manage countertransference reactions, perhaps especially challenging ones, in a mindful way.

Mindfulness practice also fosters awareness and observation of internal contents – feelings, thoughts, and body sensations as they arise – but from a non-judgmental and non-interpretive perspective. Intentionally attending to inner experience with openness and lack of judgment interrupts maladaptive thought processes and ruminations, and leads to a change of perspective and a shift in one's relationship to thoughts and emotions that include increased perspective, objectivity and calmness (Shapiro et al., 2006). Mindfulness enables us to observe our mental commentary about our experiences and see the present situation as it is rather than acting in an automatic or reactive way.

Davis and Hayes (2011) reviewed research on the positive benefits of mindfulness relevant to the practice of psychotherapy and concluded that there is evidence that mindfulness helps people to become less reactive and improves emotional regulation. Davis and Hayes also reviewed research relevant to the impact of mindfulness meditation on therapists' practices and concluded that the small number of studies in this area suggest that mindfulness practices may lead to decreased stress and anxiety, and support therapist empathy and compassion.

A small interview study with six experienced therapists who practised mindfulness meditation found that the therapists believed that mindfulness enhanced their awareness and management of their countertransference reactions (Millon & Halewood, 2015). This included increased attention to and awareness of reactions to clients and to themselves, a compassionate and curious attitude to countertransference reactions, a more compassionate attitude to themselves, and an increased ability to hold difficult emotions. The therapists believed that this then contributed to an enhanced ability to connect with clients and a deepening of therapeutic relationships. Hence, there is some promising evidence that mindfulness meditation may assist therapists to develop a relationship with their inner experience that will assist in containing and responding to countertransference reactions. Certainly, there is now substantial evidence that regular mindfulness meditation practice increases positive feelings, decreases negative ruminations and negative feelings, and assists with stress and anxiety (Davis & Hayes, 2011). It seems likely then that many therapists will benefit from mindfulness meditation practices and that in time these practices can support the therapist in managing the impact of countertransference and promote self-care.

Developing formulations to aid conceptualisation

This section is a reminder of the importance of therapists developing a formulation or conceptualisation of their patterns of relating to others. My four-step approach employs the concepts of self and other representations, the cognitive-affective reactions evoked by the triggering of these self–other representations, and the strategies used to cope with the emotional reactions. Therapists can use other concepts for formulating their relationship templates. A CBT therapist may use core and intermediate beliefs and the CBT five-part model, as in the previous chapter. Cognitive Analytic Therapists (CATs) could use the concepts of reciprocal roles and reciprocal role procedures (RRPs) (Ryle, 1998). This self-formulation, like the formulation of clients' presenting problems, may be refined over time with increasing awareness and insight into one's own sensitivities and issues.

It is also important to begin the process of formulating the clients' templates for relationships from the first contact. As discussed earlier, we can begin to formulate our ideas about these patterns by listening closely to the client and how they think and feel about themselves and others, and themselves in relationship to others. As a client tells the stories of their childhood and adult experiences of being with and relating to others, we can attend to the relationship themes that are emerging in these stories. This allows us to think on our feet when we experience a countertransference reaction.

To understand this further, we can reconsider the interaction between Meena and Joanne. Meena acted on her countertransference reaction of irritation with Joanne by making the verbal statement, 'Perhaps you are better off without him!'. She realised this later when she noted Joanne's withdrawal from her and asked her about it. However, with some more preparation, Meena may have been able to manage this better. She could have reflected on Joanne's whiny-ness earlier in sessions: Was Joanne experienced as whiny as a child? What types of relationship events were associated with Joanne's whiny-ness? Did she feel hurt, rejected, unheard? Whiny-ness also suggests perhaps some type of powerlessness. In what ways might Joanne have felt powerless as a child? And how might this relate to her going around in circles? Meena could also consider:

- What self–other representations were triggered for Joanne when she was being whiny?
- What self–other representations were triggered for her when she was feeling irritated by Joanne's whiny-ness and her going around in circles?

Once Meena has worked through this and developed some hypotheses, she is in a stronger position to be able to make sense of her own reactions and respond more empathically to Joanne the next time a similar issue emerges.

Containing the emotions – shifting back into the Adult

As we've discussed, countertransference reactions vary. Some are intense and associated with significant physiological and emotional arousal and feel difficult to contain. Strong negative reactions such as anger, dislike, disgust, or fear may be most challenging for therapists. Some countertransference reactions also feel as if they are based on truth and professional judgment when, in fact, the unconscious elements of our reactions are not recognised nor understood.

The aim, as discussed above, is to recognise as much as possible the quality of the emotions, and the thoughts/urges that go with them, and then to contain these in order to not act on them (or engage in countertransference behaviours).

Some therapists and trainees who have completed training in the four-step approach talk about the usefulness of the PAC model in helping them to contain and manage their reactions. As one therapist wrote, 'Bringing in the TA model, alongside transference and countertransference, helped me with the concept or strategy of returning to the Adult self when noticing my countertransference so as not to enact it' (Cartwright & Read, 2011, p. 52).

To illustrate this, we will return to the case of Noah and his first session with Janet and Rob. This is the first time I have introduced the PAC model's use with more than one client. This can be very useful for thinking about countertransference reactions in relation to couples and also families. Figure 6.1 below represents Noah's response to Janet and to Rob. You will notice that I have used a PAC model for Janet, Rob, and therapist Noah.

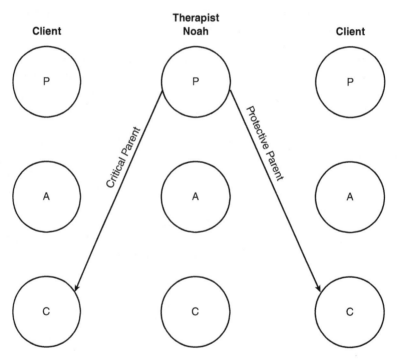

Figure 6.1 A critical Parent countertransference to Janet and a protective Parent countertransference to Rob

Figure 6.1 represents Noah's shift into a critical Parent position in relation to Janet as she cried about her relationship with Rob, and into a protective Parent position in relation to Rob during these interactions. When Noah became aware that he was being triggered into an old pattern of relating, he encouraged himself to move back into his Adult in relation to both clients and was able to do this.

It is also possible, however, that Noah may struggle to return to the Adult position and may continue to feel triggered into a critical or protective parental position at times during sessions. However, he can remind himself to return to the Adult. It may also assist Noah if he combines this with taking some deep breaths and is compassionate to himself and practises his mindfulness strategies.

Adopting an empathic attitude towards the client and self

Adopting an empathic attitude towards the client is likely to assist the therapist to move back into the Adult therapist position and respond to the client from this position. Having developed a conceptualisation or formulation of the client's history of relationships and patterns of relating to others will assist the therapist in adopting an empathic attitude. We often feel more empathic towards clients if we think about what a client has been through in life to bring them to this moment. Meena, for example, completed the reflective practice activity and realised that she had not thought about the meaning of Joanne's whining. Following this exercise, she spent some time reflecting on what she knew of Joanne's childhood. As the youngest of three girls, she often felt powerless when it came to any competition or conflict between them. As she said, 'I could never win no matter what I tried. I used to get upset and cry and then I was called a cry-baby, or else I would get really angry and try to hit them or kick them and they would just hold me at arm's length and mock me'. When Joanne got upset and told her parents, she was usually told not to be a 'sook' or to not 'take things to heart'. At school, too, Joanne was one of the smallest girls in the class and tended to feel overpowered by the other girls and their reactions.

Meena then reflected on Joanne's self–other representations. She considered these:

- Self as powerless/others as powerful
- Self as needy/others as withholding
- Self as lonely/others as unavailable or rejecting
- Self as ineffective/others as judgmental.

The emotions associated with these self–other representations may have been hurt, anger, fear, loneliness, and powerlessness. Whiny-ness could result from feelings of powerlessness and frustration – of not being able to have what one wants or needs as others are withholding and critical. These are hypotheses that may help Meena contain her reaction to Joanne's whiny-ness. These hypotheses can also guide her interventions.

Empathic self-talk

Therapists can use self-talk to support themselves to be able to move back into the Adult. This can focus on empathy for the client and empathy or compassion for one's self. For example, Meena could say to herself:

> I'm feeling like Joanne is beginning to whine again. I find clients' whining a bit painful for me. It triggers me somehow and that's just what it is. I can recognise it for what it is.

It does mean something is happening for Joanne that is difficult for her. She's had so many experiences of feeling powerless and feeling like she cannot have what she needs and wants.

Just stay calm and breathe and focus on Joanne and what is happening for her at the moment.

Hence, Meena has made use of her conceptualisation of Joanne and her self–other representations to bring herself back into an empathic position in relation to Joanne. She has also been kind to herself.

Checking hypotheses with clients

Throughout this book, we have talked about developing hypotheses about the interpersonal processes that happen between ourselves and our clients. This process rests on the notion that countertransference is a tool that can provide insight into the client's subjective experiences in therapy. In Step Three of the four-step process, we examine the interpersonal processes that occur in therapy between therapist and client, and we can ask ourselves these three questions:

1. Am I responding to the client as significant others in the past have? (Complementary countertransference)
2. Am I feeling like the client is feeling now in therapy or has often felt in the past? (Concordant countertransference)
3. Is my countertransference related to my own personal issues and sensitivities? (Subjective or personal countertransference).

The therapist can then reflect on these three questions in the therapy session and then check out their hypotheses with the client. As an example of this, we can think about Andrea's experience. Andrea has been working with Ben for 8 months. Ben is married and has two children. Ben wants to separate from his wife. He came to this conclusion following couples therapy with another therapist. He tells Andrea he cares about his wife and loves his children but feels he is living a lie. He thinks his wife will be devastated and he is frightened that his 8- and 10-year-old sons will reject him. He is also worrying about his own parents and how they will react. Ben is feeling 'tied up in knots about it'.

Andrea has been feeling patient and compassionate towards Ben. She understands how life-changing this decision will be. She and Ben have been talking through his plan to talk to his wife over the last three or four sessions – how and when will Ben bring this up with his wife, what will he do if she insists he leaves the house, how will he manage himself at work over the next period, and how and when he will talk to his parents and to his children.

While Andrea has been feeling patient and compassionate towards Ben, over the last three sessions there have been brief periods of therapy when she has had quite a strong feeling of irritation, which she has experienced as in her chest. Andrea decides to work through the three questions to see if this is helpful.

1. Am I responding to the client as significant others in the past have? Andrea thinks this is possible. Ben was taught to put others first by his parents who had a strong sense of community service. When Ben branched out and did something that was against the rules, he was chided and one of the strongest criticisms was that he was being selfish. His father would sometimes not speak to him for several days when he considered that Ben had been 'selfish'. When this happened, he felt 'bad' and had a deep sense of sadness that he had disappointed his parents and lost especially his father's approval. Reflecting on the PAC model, Andrea wondered if he was experiencing her as a critical Parent and if, in some way, she had moved into a critical Parent position.

2. Am I feeling like the client is feeling now in therapy or has often felt in the past?
The second question introduces the possibility that Ben is in his Child and is feeling irritated with Andrea or with the interactions between them. Could he be feeling towards her as he felt towards his parents when they chastised him? Is she identifying with his child-like anger?

3. Is my countertransference related to my own sensitivities or personal issues?
Andrea has been here with some other clients – different situations but similar challenges. Usually, she has helped clients with this and been patient with the process so she is unsure if there is something about this situation in particular that is triggering for her personally.

In reflecting on each of these questions, Andrea's overall hypothesis is that Ben's self–other representation of self as bad/selfish and other as critical has been triggered and Ben is responding to her as a critical Parent.

One way of checking this out is to ask Ben how he has been feeling when she has had these countertransference feelings. Andrea decides to check in with Ben and see how he is feeling next time she has these irritable sensations.

Checking in with the client

Halfway through the next session, Andrea once again experiences these shoots of irritation in her chest. They seem to come out of the blue and she is not aware of having felt irritated before this. This happens as Ben is talking about when he is going to talk to his wife. He has decided how he is going to do this and what he is going to say. But he is having trouble working out the best time.

Andrea takes the opportunity to raise this with Ben as he pauses in his conversation. Andrea tries to speak gently and also a little slower as she realises she will be interrupting Ben's train of thought.

Andrea: Ben, I'm just wondering. [Pause] Over the last while you have been thinking through when to speak to Anika. I'm wondering how you have been feeling as you have been talking about this. I mean, feeling underneath … inside yourself.

[Andrea says it in this way as she wants to differentiate between how Ben feels about talking to his wife and how he feels about talking about this in session with her]

Ben: [Pause] I'm not sure. I hadn't thought about it. [Pause] I know I'm feeling a bit uncomfortable. [Pause] If I think about it, I'm feeling as if you must be getting really fed up with me going on and on about this. We've been talking about this for weeks. You must be getting really sick of it.

This partially confirms aspects of Andrea's hypotheses. Ben is thinking/feeling that she is fed up with him – this confirms partially the idea that Ben is experiencing or placing her in a critical Parent position. Put another way, this suggests that a self–other representation of self as bad/selfish and other as disappointed/critical has been triggered. This seems possible given that Ben is going to deeply disappoint his family and may feel as if he is disappointing his therapist by having difficulty moving forward. According to this hypothesis, Ben is transferring a critical/disappointed parent onto Andrea.

This also opens up the possibility of a new conversation for Andrea and Ben as Andrea can guide Ben to talk about what is happening between them as he tries to work through how to talk to his wife. She could use some of the strategies discussed in repairing disruptions and ruptures in the previous chapter. But first she can explore his understanding of what he is experiencing as they work together on this life-changing decision.

Developing hypotheses that attempt to explain our countertransference reactions in terms of what might be happening for the client in session, and checking these out with the client, is one of the main ways that we can use our countertransference as a tool in therapy. If Andrea was unable to come up with a hypothesis, she could still ask the client what he is feeling as they talk about his decision and this might provide her with some insight into her countertransference and what is happening for Ben. If it becomes clear that there is a disruption to their relationship, then she can use the strategies discussed in the previous chapter and talk this through with Ben. This might then lead to Ben gaining deeper insight into his own responses and may also aid him in his decision-making process in regard to his desire to divorce.

Developing hypotheses and checking them out with the client

Developing hypotheses that attempt to explain the interpersonal processes that are occurring in therapy and contributing to our countertransference reactions is one of the main ways that we can use our countertransference as a tool in therapy.

In the next section, we turn to the topic of sexual countertransference. As we consider these therapist experiences, we will reflect again on the strategies that can be used to manage countertransference feelings, including sexual feelings.

Sexual countertransference

Research suggests that most therapists have experienced sexual attraction towards a client. Sonne and Jochai (2014), for example, reviewed previous survey research in this area and concluded that the majority of therapists reported having experienced sexual attraction to at least one client. A much smaller group reported having engaged in some form of sexual activity with clients. Therapists who did engage in sexual contact with a client were more likely to be male, more experienced therapists, older than their clients, and more likely to be going through a difficult period in their lives. It is also very disappointing and sad to note that there is some evidence that clients who experienced incest as children are among the group of clients at risk of sexual boundary violations from therapists (Broden & Agresti, 1998).

Experienced therapists and researchers with expertise and knowledge in this area emphasise the importance of therapists and trainees seeking supervision or consultation if sexual attraction is present in sessions because of the heightened risks to clients, therapists, and therapy progress. However, sex and sexual feelings generally are something of a taboo subject. Sexual experience is a human domain that we tend to be protective of and keep private. As you will see, however, it becomes clear that it is essential for therapists and trainees to seek supervision or consultation about sexual attraction in therapy.

Sexual attraction and sexual countertransference

Sexual countertransference is used generally to refer to the sexual or erotic feelings that therapists have towards clients, and sexual transference is used to refer to the sexual or erotic feelings that clients have towards therapists. Gelso, Pérez Rojas and Marmarosh (2014) suggest that it is important for therapists to differentiate between sexual attraction that occurs within the real relationship, and sexual countertransference. Therapists are likely to come across clients who are similar to the type of person/s they are attracted to in everyday life, and some clients, because of their beauty or attractiveness, may be experienced as attractive by many other people in their lives. In order to think about the implications of this, consider the following case.

Pause and reflect: Jason's experience of immediate attraction

Jason, a therapist with 12 years' experience, instantly found Bobbie attractive. He saw him sitting in the waiting room and thought, 'Wow, he is gorgeous'. Jason was not aware at that moment that Bobbie was his new client. When Bobbie was ushered into the room by the receptionist, Jason felt himself 'go pink', as he said to his supervisor at their next session. Jason was embarrassed at his response to Bobbie although he thought that Bobbie had not noticed. When Bobbie began to talk about his problems and why he had sought therapy, Jason was able to focus on what Bobbie was saying and his alertness to Bobbie's physical attractiveness subsided. He was relieved about this. After his client had left, he came across a colleague–friend in the lunch room. The friend smiled and made a comment about how good-looking Jason's client was. In reflecting on his reaction to Bobbie, Jason realised that in different non-therapy circumstances, and before he met his current partner, he might have come on to Bobbie and then felt guilty for thinking and feeling this.

1. What do you think and feel about Jason's sexual attraction to Bobbie?
2. If you had an immediate attraction to a client, what would you think and feel?
3. How can Jason keep himself and his client safe from sexual acting out?

Jason is going to work with a client who fits his idea of a very attractive male. In the next session, Bobbie talks to Jason about the number of men who come on to him and how this is leading to trust issues for him – 'They are not interested in me. They are just interested in my body', he says. Listening to Bobbie's story leads Jason to see Bobbie's vulnerable self, and when Jason has moments of attraction in the session, he is able to focus back on Bobbie, what he has been through in life, and what had brought him to therapy. However, Jason's attraction to Bobbie may be more challenging to manage if Jason's own unresolved issues or unmet needs are triggered or if Bobbie shows romantic or sexual interest in Jason.

SEXUAL COUNTERTRANSFERENCE AND THE NEEDS OF THE THERAPIST

Sexual countertransference becomes problematic if the therapist's own needs – for example, admiration, intimacy, dependence – are activated in relation to a client. In order to think about this, let us consider the case of Annette, a 40-year-old therapist who has been single for four years and, as she tells her closest friends, would really like to have a partner who loved her and whom she could love.

Annette had been working with Frederick for six sessions and they had contracted for a further 10 sessions. Annette felt a lot of empathy for Frederick. He had lost his twin sister in an accident three years ago and he was still trying, as he put it, to get back on his feet. His sister and he were very close and spent a lot of time together and he felt alone since she died. Just prior to the accident, Frederick and his sister had talked about the need for them to depend less on each other and to find partners. At the time, Frederick had actually just met someone he really liked and was dating but the loss of his sister meant that he could not be there for this woman and so they drifted apart.

Frederick was an IT person and Annette found him really intelligent, which she liked. She also thought he had a quirky sense of humour and admired his casual but elegant style of dressing. She found him easy to relate to and looked forward to their sessions. Around the eighth session, Annette realised she was dressing more carefully on the days that Frederick had a session. Then, three weeks later, Frederick cancelled due to illness and Annette felt really disappointed, and, around this time, she had a dream in which she and Frederick were holding and comforting each other. Annette decided that she needed to talk to her supervisor about this. Her supervisor was older and very experienced and she felt he would be able to help her with this and not judge her. In talking to him, she realised she had not been conscious of her growing attraction to Frederick and that she had been sympathetic to Frederick and had not been challenging him. For example, Frederick had talked two or three times about a woman in his book club that he was attracted to but said he was not quite ready for another relationship yet. In talking to her supervisor, Annette realised she had accepted this as fully valid and had not explored this with Frederick as she would normally do. She realised too that she was experiencing brief mental images of her and Frederick having breakfast together in the sun and walking on the beach holding hands.

In this situation, Annette's needs for intimacy may have been activated along with her attraction to Frederick. Annette is in a more vulnerable situation than Jason, in some ways. Jason is more physically attracted to his client but he is readily able to focus back on Bobbie's vulnerabilities and needs. Jason is also in a stable and caring relationship. Annette is experiencing attraction to Frederick and her own needs for intimacy and care are being activated, leading to fantasies of partnering with Frederick. She had also engaged in some countertransference behaviour although she did not recognise this as such – she had been dressing up more on the days of his appointments, and she had been overly sympathetic to Frederick and had not encouraged him to consider the issues around approaching the woman in his book club to whom he was attracted. When she thought about Frederick having a new partner, she realised she felt a little jealous and then she felt really guilty. On the other hand, Annette had a strong sense of the importance of professional and ethical behaviour and continues to take her thoughts and feelings about her client to her supervisor.

Ethical and professional issues

As discussed earlier in Chapter 2, codes of ethics and professional guidelines prohibit sexual relationships with clients, and therapists who engage in boundary violations are at risk of losing their rights to practise. The UK Council for Psychotherapy's *Code of Ethics and Professional Practice* (2019), for example, under the Best Interests of Clients states that a practitioner must: '1. Act in your client's best interests. 2. Treat clients with respect. 3. Respect your client's autonomy. 4. Not have sexual contact or sexual relationship with clients. 5. Not exploit or abuse your relationship with clients (current or past) for any purpose including your emotional, sexual or financial gain' (UK Council for Psychotherapy, 2019, p. 1).

Celenza (2017), a psychoanalytic psychotherapist, makes the important point that therapists must preserve the therapeutic (or analytic) space, which is characterised by an appropriate asymmetrical primary focus of care and attention towards clients and their needs. Violations of the boundaries within the therapeutic space reveal to the client the therapist's willingness 'to lie or dissemble', and the promise of the safe therapeutic space is broken (Celenza, 2017, p. 159).

Evidence of the effects of these violations on clients was found in a survey of previous clients whose therapists had engaged in sexual misconduct (Eichenberg, Becker-Fischer, & Fischer, 2010). Most participants in the study stated that the therapist initiated the contact and the majority reported an exacerbation of their emotional and psychological problems and a decline in overall wellbeing. Many had had to seek further therapy to deal with the negative effects.

Sexual transference

Sometimes clients are sexually attracted to their therapists. Once again, as with sexual countertransference, the nature, intensity, and frequency of the experience of attraction will vary, as will the meaning of it. Some clients may at times feel some attraction to the therapist and wish they could be part of the therapist's life but not experience any negative impact of this and see it as a normal reaction to an attractive and empathic person. It is also important for therapists to be aware that therapy creates an intimate situation between client and therapist in which the therapist encourages the client to talk about their most personal concerns and responds in an empathic and caring way.

You will recall that Freud warned psychoanalysts about the dangers of 'transference love' and reminded his readers that clients' attraction to them was to do with the conditions of psychoanalysis and not to do with the analyst's attractive attributes:

He (the analyst) must recognize that the patient's falling in love is induced by the analytic situation and is not to be attributed to the charms of his own person. (Freud, 1993, p. 174)

Approximately a third of therapists reported that they thought at least one client had been sexually attracted to them (Koocher & Keith-Spiegel, 2016). Occasionally, a client may reveal their attraction to a therapist. They may do this because it is on their minds and the therapist has encouraged them to be open with them about how therapy is going for them. This does not mean they wish the therapist to act on this in a sexual way. Alternatively, a client could suggest a joint activity outside of therapy ('Could we have a coffee together sometime?', 'Is there any chance that when we end our sessions, we could spend some time together?'), or give a clear indication that they would like to have a romantic and/or sexual relationship with the therapist ('I find you so attractive. I can't get my mind off you. I feel like you are the right person for me').

This can be really challenging for us as therapists, and it is especially challenging for therapists when they find the client attractive and are having difficulty managing their own reactions. In the next section, we will discuss some ideas for how to manage sexual countertransference, including how to manage situations such as the above.

Managing sexual countertransference

As discussed earlier, codes of ethics prohibit engaging in sexual activity with clients. While it is important and helpful that therapists understand and respect the need for this boundary, managing strong sexual attraction and, perhaps in some instances, feelings of love, can be challenging, especially when a therapist is caught up in these emotional and physiological responses in therapy situations.

The four-step approach to understanding and managing your countertransference reactions will assist you in this endeavour.

The first step is to be aware of any early signs of sexual countertransference. Jason's response to Bobbie was immediate and he was conscious of it. Annette's sexual countertransference was subtler and, by the sixth session, her unconscious reaction to Frederick was impacting on her therapeutic effectiveness. While Annette had not broken any boundaries with Frederick, it is important that she became aware of the early signs and her subtle countertransference behaviours. Once a therapist has become aware of sexual attraction to a client, and/or a client's attraction to him or her, it is essential to seek supervision or consultation with a trusted, experienced supervisor.

The second step is formulating the client's self and other representations and the associated emotions and defences, or coping strategies. (As noted earlier, therapists can also do this formulation using the concepts from their favoured therapeutic approach.) Understanding the client's vulnerabilities and therapeutic needs that have developed from within their history of relationships will assist the therapist to manage the sexual attraction. Jason did not have time to do this before experiencing his strong sexual attraction to Bobbie. However, he began to do this in the first session as Bobbie talked about the ways that he felt treated by men. Jason begins to hypothesise that Bobbie may have experienced a history of being sexualised by others and thinks that he must also check Bobbie's abuse history. This focused him on his client's needs.

The third step is understanding how the sexual transference or sexual countertransference may be emerging within the therapeutic relationship. To illustrate this, we can think about Annette's response to Frederick. Over the sessions, it became clearer that Frederick and his sister Frances became close, and almost clung to each other throughout their childhood to cope with their father's alcoholism and aggression towards their mother. Their mother was depressed and cried a lot and their father became even angrier. Frederick and Frances clung to each other as children and as teenagers, and as young adults became each other's best friend. This tended to get in the way of some other friendships and relationships, which was why they had decided to try to be more independent of each other not long before Frances was killed.

When Annette and her supervisor were exploring her sexual attraction and talked through Frederick's childhood, her supervisor made this comment:

Supervisor: So when Frances died, Frederick was devastated. He could barely get out of bed and she was gone so he had no-one to turn to or felt he did?

Annette: Yes, and it must have been frightening for him. He did talk about how he used to talk to his sister at night when he was in bed and how that sometimes gave him comfort but at other times he felt 'broken up'.

Supervisor: I am reminded of the dream you talked about two weeks ago.

Annette: [Pause, Annette feels embarrassed and guilty. Embarrassed that she may have been desiring comfort from a client and guilty that she is putting these feelings onto Frederick] Yes, I had a dream of us comforting each other. It felt good. [Pause] I feel really bad about it.

Supervisor: Well, it's an important dream, Annette. And it drew your attention to something that was happening for you in relation to Frederick. I think that it was quite helpful that you had that dream.

Annette: Yes, that's true. It did bring it to my consciousness.

Supervisor: Can you say what the 'it' is, Annette?

Annette: I guess that I was starting to have romantic feelings towards Frederick – that he could be a good partner for me.

Supervisor: OK. So it's important to have recognised that. And, as you know, it happens to most of us at some time. We meet a client we would be attracted to in real life and then perhaps the intensity of the sessions, and the empathy we feel for the client grows, and clients can start to have warm feelings towards us as well. I wonder what is happening for Frederick? I wonder what he is feeling towards you?

Annette: I suppose he could be having similar feelings towards me. He does smile at me sweetly sometimes. He is wanting/needing comfort. Like we talked about, he and Frances sort of merged together to cope.

Supervisor: And needs for comfort and intimacy can become sexualised – and it sounds as if you and he might have been attracted to each other in real life. So maybe he is having romantic or sexual feelings towards you. Perhaps this even came first and you have been, at least in part, responding to a pull from him?

Annette: The thought of it frightens me. It's difficult enough coping with my own feelings but having to cope with his too.

Supervisor: Well, let's talk about that.

The fourth step relates to managing the countertransference reaction. The first strategy that Annette can use is to notice when she is experiencing a sexual countertransference to Frederick and prompting herself to 'Move back into your Adult'. Annette prefers to say to herself: 'Move into your Wise Therapist self'. As Annette does this, she takes some deep breaths and brings her breath to an even pace. She can then shift to an empathic position in relation to herself and to the client. This helps with staying in the Wise Therapist self. Annette says to herself: 'It's OK to feel like this. I understand where it's coming from. I can re-focus on Frederick and what he needs. He seems to be looking sad. I wonder what is happening for him at the moment'.

Annette's challenge, however, deepens when, towards the end of the twelfth session, Frederick says to her:

Frederick: Annette. I have something I need to say to you. I don't feel good about it but I feel like I have to be honest with you.

Annette: That's OK, Frederick. What is it?

Frederick: I've started having feelings for you and I can't concentrate on what we are talking about. [Pause] I feel attracted to you. I think if we had met outside of here, I would feel the same. [Frederick waits for a response]

One of the mistakes that therapists can make at this point is to quickly state the ethical and professional boundaries and unwittingly shame the client. For example, Frederick would likely be wounded if Annette said:

Annette: [Strangled voice] Well, Frederick, I can't have any type of relationship with you, other than as your therapist, as this would be against my professional ethics and I could get into trouble if I did.

He would experience Annette as a critical Parent. Instead, Annette says:

Annette: It's important for you to tell me about things that are affecting you in therapy, Frederick. [Pause] Can you tell me some more of what you have been thinking about this?

Frederick: I've been thinking that, if we were together, I would feel whole again. I think I need a relationship with someone like you. You are intelligent and warm. And I feel like you might be a bit lonely yourself?

Annette: Perhaps I am sometimes Frederick. [Smiles gently] Can you tell me a bit more about feeling whole again – what that would mean to you?

Frederick: I've been feeling like I am not really myself since my sister died. It's getting a bit better. Sometimes I do feel whole. But I feel that with someone like you I would feel whole again and we could be good for each other.

Annette: It's important to me Frederick that I am here to help you find a life that feels good for you – where you will feel whole more of the time.

And I know that you have been really wanting someone to be close to and therapy is quite an intimate situation. Therapists are there for their clients in ways that often doesn't happen in normal life. So it is special in some ways.

[Annette was feeling calmer than she had been. She took another breath and reminded herself to remain in her Wise Therapist self. She decided to bring the topic back to Frederick and his needs]

Annette: Frederick, this feeling of wanting to be whole again, and have someone you can feel that with. Is it just me or are you also having some of these feelings towards anyone else in your life?

Frederick: Well, maybe to Jill. I still like her and we seem to get on well but I don't think I want a relationship with her. I'm not sure I could handle it.

Annette: But you are still attracted to her?

Frederick: Yes.

Annette: [Speaks in a gentle tone] Perhaps I feel a little safer than Jill, as it's not really possible with me but it might be possible with her?

Frederick: [Smiles nervously] Maybe there's something in that.

In this excerpt above, Annette has been careful not to shame Frederick. She calmed herself following her initial fear reaction. Then she asked Frederick to say something more about what he was thinking and feeling. She had already discussed with her supervisor the possibility of Frederick's attraction to her being based, in part, on his dependency needs and needs for intimacy. She also recognised that there is likely some realistic attraction between them as people.

After asking him about his thoughts and feelings, she takes it back to his needs and what is happening for him in this regard in his life outside therapy. This is helpful as Frederick is able to acknowledge his attraction to Jill who is, in fact, available. At the end of the session, Annette says:

Annette: How are you feeling about what we've talked about today?

Frederick: I'm still feeling embarrassed but I am also feeling a bit better and I'm glad that I told you. I think it will help me to focus on whatever we are talking about and that has not really been happening.

Annette: That's good, Frederick. I'm glad.

As you will have noted, Annette did not reveal that she also had some feelings of attraction to Frederick. Some experienced therapists who have written about sexual countertransference recommend that therapists do not reveal their own sexual feelings towards a client, as this can be detrimental for the client (e.g., Gabbard, 2017; Gelso et al., 2014). As Gelso et al. wrote,

> Particularly with regard to sexual feelings, our view is that these are best not shared with the patient, as sharing them adds a special and needless burden on the patient, and impedes rather than facilitates patient exploration of both his or her inner and relational world. (2014, p. 129)

As with any decisions in therapy, the therapist ideally focuses on clients' needs and what is likely to be helpful for them.

In the final section of this chapter, we turn to issues related to sharing countertransference reactions with clients, including the pros and cons.

Sharing countertransference reactions with clients

There are important reasons for therapists to be cautious about sharing or revealing their countertransference reactions to clients as they occur in sessions. Therapists are not always aware of the nature of countertransference reactions at any given moment and the meaning of these within the therapeutic relationship and therapy context. Therapists may also be emotionally aroused and express their countertransference reaction in a way that impacts negatively on the client and the therapeutic alliance. On the other hand, therapists do disclose aspects of themselves, their lives outside therapy, and their reactions within therapy contexts, and this can also be helpful and deepen the relationship.

Self-disclosure

The term 'therapist self-disclosure' is somewhat confusing as the term in itself could represent therapist disclosures about themselves including that of coun- tertransference feelings. However, in a meta-analysis of research into therapist self-disclosure (TSD), Hill, Knox, and Pinto-Coelho (2018) used the term TSD to refer to therapists' verbal statements about some aspect of themselves or their lives *outside* therapy. Examples of therapist self-disclosure include: 'I had quite a lot of difficulty studying too when I began university', 'I get annoyed too when other cars push in front of me, like that', 'I found in the past that it took me a year or two to really settle into a new role'. TSDs tend to be brief and not generate much further discussion. The therapy session tends to shift back to what the client and therapist were discussing (Hill et al., 2018).

An interview study with experienced therapists revealed that the therapists used TSDs to provide support for clients and to normalise and demonstrate empathy and understanding for their experiences (Pinto-Coelho et al., 2018). Successful TSDs do provide benefits and can enhance the therapeutic relation- ship and client wellbeing (Hill et al., 2018). However, TSDs can also be expe- rienced negatively by clients. In the interview study, unsuccessful TSDs were often preceded by therapist countertransference reactions to the client (Pinto- Coelho et al., 2018). The therapists also thought they had misjudged the con- tent or timing of the TSDs that were experienced as unhelpful by clients. The authors concluded that TSDs worked best when therapists were accurately attuned to clients, assessed the timing of the TSD, chose a TSD that was com- fortably received by the client and experienced as helpful, and managed their countertransference reactions.

Immediacy

In their meta-analysis, Hill and colleagues (2018) also examined the research on therapists' use of 'Immediacy' (Im). They defined Im as therapist discus- sions with clients about their relationship as it occurs in the here-and-now. Therapists use Im to encourage clients to express their feelings and thoughts about the therapist/therapy, to process what is happening between themselves and their clients, and to repair any disruptions or ruptures. Therapists in this book have used these strategies on a number of occasions, including the exam- ples that were discussed in Chapter 5, which examined the processes related to repairing alliance ruptures. For example, Joan expressed her feeling of con- cern for Ana. She drew on her countertransference and aimed to put this into words in a way that would be acceptable to Ana.

Joan: Yes, I remember you said that you had a busy period coming up. I did think about that when I was unwell and had to cancel our appointment. I was a bit concerned that it would be hard for you – my cancelling.

Meena acted out on her countertransference reaction of annoyance with her client in an earlier session, noted the change in her client, reflected on this, and decided to bring this into the session.

Meena: Joanne, I think I've noticed – tell me if I am wrong – that you do not seem to be quite as involved in therapy as you were before. I've noticed in the last few minutes of last week and today that you seem unhappy or unsure about something, perhaps what we are talking about? Or I'm wondering if there is something I have done that is bothering you?

These can be helpful strategies that lead to an exploration of the therapeutic relationship and deepen the therapeutic alliance. On the other hand, clients are not always comfortable with therapists' talking openly, sharing their reactions, and asking them to do the same. Once again, it seems important that therapists are also aware of their motivations and are not acting on countertransference feelings or urges.

Sharing countertransference reactions

From my perspective, the most valuable use of countertransference is as a tool to gain insight into clients' experiences and aid understanding of the interpersonal processes that are occurring between therapists and clients. However, as noted above, it is likely that therapists will at times decide to share something of their countertransference reactions or feelings with clients in order to open up a conversation about what is happening between them. This can also be helpful as therapy progresses and the client is becoming more aware of their own patterns of relating to others, including the therapist. Prior to doing this, it is important that therapists have processed their countertransference feelings, and actively considered if sharing the reaction with the client represents a wise therapeutic decision or is motivated by the urge to express the feelings.

Sharing a countertransference feeling: Have I shifted back into the Adult?

To assist with this, therapists can ask themselves if they are in the Adult position as they consider revealing a personal reaction to a client. If the therapist has been triggered – either by an internal trigger or a trigger in the therapy situation – into either a Parent or Child self, and has not been able to shift back into Adult, it may be wiser to not act on the urge at this point in the session.

Supervisors and teachers are often hesitant or cautious in their recommendations to supervisees or trainees in this regard, as am I. This is likely to be based on experience that interventions that involve sharing a countertransference reaction or asking a client to open up about how they are feeling towards the therapist or therapy, can have some negative consequences unless the timing is right, the words capture the desired meaning, and the client is ready and able to receive this type of communication. On the other hand, experienced therapists from many therapeutic approaches share their contained and processed reactions with clients when they judge this will be helpful. Often this expression, however, will be in a modified form, as demonstrated by the examples provided throughout.

Summary

This chapter examined a number of areas related to managing countertransference in practice. These have included ways in which therapists can increase their awareness of their reactions to clients including the practice of mindfulness meditation, and the use of reflective practice exercises between client sessions. Developing formulations of the client's templates for relationships (e.g., self–other representations, core beliefs about self and other) can assist therapists to understand and conceptualise their countertransference reactions as they arise in sessions.

We then considered strategies for managing countertransference reactions as they emerge. These included calming strategies such as breathing techniques or mindfulness practices, using empathic self-talk, and encouraging the self to move back into the Adult or the Wise Therapist self. Therapists can later check their hypotheses about the transference and countertransference processes that may be happening with the client by using an inquiring approach when these experiences emerge again in sessions. The chapter then discussed issues related to managing sexual countertransference in a way that protects and preserves the therapeutic relationship, and issues related to sharing countertransference reactions with clients.

Recommended readings

Blonna, R. (2014). An Acceptance Commitment Therapy approach to sexual attraction. In M. Luca, *Sexual attraction in therapy: Clinical perspectives on moving beyond the taboo: A guide for training and practice* (pp. 80–96). Hoboken, NJ: John Wiley and Sons.

Cartwright, C., Hayes, J. A., Yang, Y., & Shires, A. (2021). 'Thinking it through': Toward a model of reflective practice for trainee psychologists' countertransference reactions. *Australian Psychologist, 56,* 168–180.

Gelso, C. J., Pérez Rojas, A. E., & Marmarosh, C. (2014). Love and sexuality in the therapeutic relationship. *Journal of Clinical Psychology, 70,* 123–134.

Hill, C. E., Knox, S., & Pinto-Coelho, K. G. (2018). Therapist self-disclosure and immediacy: A qualitative meta-analysis. *Psychotherapy, 55,* 445–460.

Kabat-Zinn, J. (2003). Mindfulness-based interventions in context: Past, present, and future. *Clinical Psychology: Science and Practice, 10,* 144–156.

Sonne, J. L. & Jochai, D. (2014). The 'vicissitudes of love' between therapist and patient: A review of the research on romantic and sexual feelings, thoughts, and behaviors in psychotherapy. *Journal of Clinical Psychology, 70,* 182–195.

7
Classroom and Group Learning and Countertransference

Most of the teaching and learning activities that I have engaged in with therapists and trainees have been conducted in groups – either in workshops with therapists, or in classroom teaching and in group supervision. This chapter discusses the benefits and risks inherent in discussing countertransference in group situations and includes ideas for establishing safety and enhancing learning. The chapter provides an overview of reflective practice activities that are based on the four-step approach (Chapters 3 and 4) and can be used in classroom and group situations. The activities are designed to support colleagues to work together to enhance understanding and management of countertransference. The activities described in this chapter can also be used in supervision.

Risks and benefits of group reflections

There are a number of potential benefits to reflecting on countertransference with a group of colleagues and with a facilitator or supervisor. These include:

- learning from others' experiences
- benefiting from others' perspectives
- experiencing validation and empathy
- hearing about others' countertransference reactions to the client.

These in turn can lead to increased:

- acceptance of countertransference feelings and thoughts
- openness to talking about countertransference
- attunement to countertransference reactions
- ability to conceptualise and manage countertransference.

On the other hand, care has to be taken when therapists talk openly about their countertransference experiences, particularly in group situations, and especially in the early stages of learning about and becoming comfortable with countertransference.

Therapists often feel vulnerable when talking about their countertransference reactions. As therapists talk about their therapeutic work with clients, they hold both their clients' vulnerabilities and their own. It is important then that classrooms and group situations are safe places that provide support and containment for therapists and their clients. This requires thoughtful discussion within a group in order to establish group practices that will help to avoid some of the problems that can emerge. Consider, for example, the case example below.

Pause and reflect: A case example

Bronwyn was in group supervision with a clinical supervisor and three other colleagues all of whom were recent graduates from training programmes. Bronwyn was talking about her client Davina's behaviour in therapy and the negative countertransference reaction she was having towards Davina. Davina was often late, then wanted to extend the session and was annoyed when she could not. On two recent occasions, Davina had made comments on Bronwyn's clothing ('You've got your hippy dress on today', 'Looking swish today! Got a big date?'). As Bronwyn was talking about this, another therapist in the group said, 'OMG, how do you cope with her behaviour! That is so rude and disrespectful! You'll have to set some boundaries for her'.

1. What, if anything, might be helpful about the therapist's reaction to Bronwyn's story?
2. How might the therapist's reaction be problematic?
3. What do you think might underlie the therapist's reaction to Bronwyn's client?

As you can see from above, a therapist has reacted strongly to the client's behaviour as described by Bronwyn. It is possible that Bronwyn might find this reaction normalising as it validates her feelings of frustration. She may also know the therapist well and understand that this is her way of expressing empathy and support. On the other hand, the therapist's reaction is uncontained, interrupts Bronwyn's flow, and seems critical. The therapist giving feedback appears to have shifted into her critical Parent either in relation to the client, Bronwyn, or both. In some instances, group members' reactions to other therapists' clients can lead therapists to feel protective of the client and/or themselves, become less confident about sharing, and withdraw.

Over the years, I have seen a number of situations that have been difficult for therapists and trainees presenting their work. These include group members:

- laughing about or making fun of a client
- being critical of the therapist or client
- overwhelming the therapist with questions
- asking questions in a challenging way
- making personal comments about the therapist's personality or personal issues
- asking for personal information.

This is why it is important to have a teacher or facilitator who can guide the discussions and help to ensure safe and supportive practices.

Working mainly with objective countertransference

When engaging in self-reflective practice, the trainee or therapist needs to consider both the objective and subjective aspects of countertransference. When working in groups, it works well to explore the objective aspects (the transference and countertransference) and leave it to the therapist as to whether they want to share their own personal contributions to what is happening. Therapists will often do this if they feel that the situation is safe. This is also something that the group can discuss as part of their preparation for working on countertransference in a group situation.

Points to discuss prior to working in groups

It can be helpful to have a supervisor or teacher available to lead countertransference reflective groups. In order to create a safe environment, group members can consider and discuss the following:

- What boundaries and practices do you want to put into place in regard to confidentiality and privacy for therapists and clients?
- How would you like others in the group to respond when you talk about your client work and your countertransference reactions?
- How do you feel about being asked questions by group members and how can this work best?
- How would you like group members to communicate with you about their own countertransference reactions to your countertransference or your client?

Once these have been discussed and agreed upon, the group can engage in a number of reflective practice activities.

Reflective practice activities

These can be done with a group of colleagues who are interested in focusing on countertransference or in classroom situations. I will introduce a number of activities below. However, the order of these activities can be changed, and you can also choose to do the activities that work best for your group.

Warm-up exercise

In order to become comfortable with talking openly about countertransference reactions, it can be helpful for everyone in the group (or sub-group) to practise sharing a recent countertransference reaction – without trying to analyse it. For example, everyone in the group who feels comfortable doing so shares a recent negative countertransference reaction, and then the group repeats this process with each sharing a positive countertransference reaction. These do not have to be discussed in detail. It is often just helpful to learn how to name countertransference reactions and is also helpful for other group members to hear that they are not the only ones having these reactions.

Sharing negative and positive countertransference reactions: examples

I was working with a client with a fear of vomiting and she described seeing vomit on a footpath and I felt really disgusted and nauseous.

I am working with a child whose mother died. Sometimes I feel so warm towards her. I just feel like picking her up and taking her home and keeping her safe.

I was sitting in on a session with another therapist and the client suddenly shouted at him about how insensitive he was. I felt shocked and I felt like a small child cowering in a corner.

I felt so sorry for my client. She's had such a difficult life, and she is so sweet to me, such a kind person. I found myself really wanting to make things better for her – I felt like I needed to help make things right for her.

Reflective practice activities and the four-step approach

The next section describes a number of reflective practice activities related to the four-step approach (Chapters 3 and 4) to do in class or in groups.

Choosing who will go first

It is helpful to begin the reflective exercises with a therapist/s who would like to talk through their countertransference reactions to a client. If the group has more than around six participants, you might want to begin with breaking into smaller groups for the discussions. In a recent teaching situation, I was working with 12 trainees, so the class broke into four groups of three trainees for the following exercises and then came back together as part of the larger group.

Beginning with the countertransference reaction and the context

The therapist who is presenting their case begins by talking about the countertransference reaction/s and the context for that. What was happening between them and the client in the therapy situation? How was the client responding? What was happening for the therapist? What were the countertransference thoughts and feelings, and what did the therapist do?

In order to bring these activities more alive, we will briefly consider an example of how this can work in a group using a case example from Naomi and her sessions with Pattie. Naomi said she would like to talk about her therapy situation and her countertransference reaction. Naomi had seen her client for six sessions.

Naomi: As yet, I can hardly get a word in edgewise. I try. My client, Pattie, says she wants help with feeling better in her life and would like people to treat her better and respect her more. She appears down and gained a moderate depression rating on a depression scale. She appears really flat and she talks in a kind of monotone and she talks on like this [illustrating a slow drawn out speech]. She talks a lot about her mother who was a solo mother and says that her mother was mean to her and really ungiving. Yesterday, I tried to make an empathic statement when she was talking about her mother. I said something like, 'It must have been really hard on you growing up Pattie'. She looked up – she's always looking down at her lap or the carpet – she looked up and said something like, 'well yes obviously' and then continued on in a type of droning voice. I feel bad saying this, but that is how it seems and there's no breaks for me to get in.

Teacher: Can you tell us some more about your countertransference reactions, Naomi? Maybe generally and also yesterday when she reacted like that.

Naomi: I've been thinking about this. I feel cut out, like I'm not there, like I'm irrelevant to her. I feel worthless actually, and a bit desperate sometimes to try to get a word in edgewise. It feels like there is no room for me. Other times I just feel a bit numb and not very engaged.

Teacher: And what thoughts were going through your head yesterday when you made the empathic statement and she said 'obviously'?

Naomi: I was thinking, what's the point. I might as well not be here. She doesn't like me and she doesn't want to hear from me. [Pause] But yet she keeps coming. She's always on time, leaves on time. I find it strange.

Teacher: Thank you Naomi. If it's okay with you, we'll talk about this now in our groups? [Naomi indicates yes] But an important question first. Where do you feel that you were in terms of the PAC model during this time? Were you in a Child, Adult or Parent? And did that change at all at the time?

Naomi: Oh, I haven't thought about it. Um, I feel like I was in the Child most of the time but I might have gone into a critical Parent for a bit and felt annoyed with her when she said 'obviously!'.

Hence, Naomi's sense of it is that she went into a Child position but perhaps also a critical Parent when Pattie said 'obviously'.

Pause and reflect: Was I in a Parent, Adult or Child?

This is an important question to ask and to ponder. The therapist presenting their work will have the best sense of whether they were in a Child, Adult or Parent state. A Child and a Parent can look quite similar to the outsider; for example, an angry therapist could be in a critical Parent or more of an angry Child (or adolescent) aspect of self. The therapist themselves will have the best sense of this.

Initial use of the PAC model

Sometimes it works well to use the PAC model first in order for an initial exploration of the interpersonal processes that occurred in the interaction described by the therapist. Once the therapist has talked about their counter-transference and how it emerged, the group members can engage in small group discussions and develop hypotheses about what is happening using the PAC model. Usually 15 minutes is sufficient for this initial discussion and then group members can present their tentative hypotheses about what is happening between therapist and client back to the larger group. The groups can consider complementary and concordant countertransference reactions. The presenting therapist listens to these ideas and can share their reflections as well. This is an engaging activity that can be very helpful for the presenting therapist and aids learning for all group members.

Below are two brief examples of explanations from different groups in the class. These are presented in a succinct way for learning purposes.

Jack: I'm happy to talk first about what we discussed. Our group really wondered about the client and where she was on the PAC model. We thought she probably did move to critical Parent when Naomi made the empathic statement and the client replied, obviously! We also wondered if the client was also in her critical Parent at other times, or perhaps a controlling Parent. The client seems to be keeping control of the situation perhaps like her mother kept control of her. But if this is the case, then the critical or controlling Parent could also be defending against or avoiding experiencing or expressing her Child. And Naomi ends up feeling pushed out or kept away.

Ana: We talked about similar possibilities. I suppose our greatest wondering was is this a concordant countertransference. Has Naomi gone into a Child place of feeling shut out and unworthy and she is picking up something about the client's Child – the feeling of being shut out and unworthy/unwanted. And we were wondering if the client is staying in that position for much of the session because of her own inner critical Parent who critiques her behaviour. We also wondered if she is transferring a rejecting mother onto Naomi and expecting that the therapist will be critical of her or perhaps not want her. We don't think she would be conscious of this though.

Developing hypotheses about the client's templates for relationships

In this activity, the therapist talks through the client's history of relationships, beginning if possible with early relationships with caregivers. The groups then reflect on this history including how the client currently relates to others, and tentatively proposes the client's self–other representations (or relationship templates) that developed from her history of relationships. Therapists from other approaches can use the concepts they prefer to work with in this exercise.

Teacher: Naomi, can you tell us some more about her relationship history starting with her earliest years, if you have that information?

Naomi: Pattie was brought up by a solo mother. Her mother was very bright apparently and had been completing a Masters degree when she became pregnant with Pattie on a one-night stand. The mother got no support from her parents who were very disapproving of her getting pregnant. Pattie says she doesn't understand why her mother kept her because she feels as if her mother has always resented her. Her mother had to give up her studies and always says she didn't reach her potential because of this. Pattie just remembers her mother as a bitter person who was rarely happy and who always seemed to resent having to do things for her. Pattie felt she was a chore – she was given food and shelter and nothing else – just coldness and criticism. Despite this lack of support as a child, Pattie's mother has expected her to be at her 'beck and call' in recent years and Pattie has tried to do this although she always feels depressed when she leaves her mother's house. In terms of other relationships, Pattie said she 'never learnt good social skills' although she does have two quite good friends from school who are very 'thoughtful' like her and they keep in touch. As she grew up, she also became closer to her grandparents who used to have her to stay and who were quite kind and showed an interest in her. Pattie now works as a laboratory assistant and is completing a science degree part time. She hopes to better herself. Pattie says she is quiet at work but gets good feedback on what she does. She thinks that people find her dull.

REFLECTING ON SELF–OTHER REPRESENTATIONS

The therapists once again break into small groups and reflect on the client's history of relationships in order to hypothesise about the client's self–other representations and defences or coping strategies. Naomi can choose to sit in on one group or perhaps move between groups. In this way, her colleagues engage in the reflective activities and she has the opportunity to listen to and reflect on their ideas.

The self–other representations that the groups propose include:

- Self as unwanted/unloved and other as rejecting
- Self as unseen/invisible and other as dismissive/invalidating
- Self as worthless and other as judgmental/condemning

There may not be complete agreement on these but there is some agreement that these hypothesised self–other representations do appear to fit with Pattie's experiences and ways of relating.

Reflecting on the processes between therapist and client

This activity allows for an integration of the reflections using the PAC model and the proposed self–other representations. What stands out initially is that Naomi's countertransference feelings and thoughts are similar to what Pattie is likely to have felt as a child – as if there was no room for her, a bit desperate to find a way in, and feeling worthless and unwanted. The countertransference then may be a concordant response in which Naomi, the therapist, identifies with the client's Child aspect (or in which Naomi identifies with a client's self-representation).

It is often useful at this point for group members to share any other ideas that seem important, and it is useful and important to hear from Naomi for her reactions to the group's hypotheses. It is also appropriate that the facilitator and group members acknowledge and thank those who have shared their countertransference reactions for their own learning and for the benefit of the group.

Moving back into the Adult

Sometimes it is also helpful for classmates or colleagues to share ideas about the activities that the therapist can use to support themselves to move back into the Adult. I often suggest that members of the group create positive statements or affirmations that the therapist could say to themselves to assist with this. See below for some examples.

Examples of empathic self-talk

In Naomi's situation I might find it helpful to say to myself something like,

Pattie has felt like this all of her life – as if there is no room for her and she is shut out, from life really. It's good that I can pick this up from her. I know now how she might have felt and still feels in her life. I can move back into my Wise Therapist Self and work at finding a way to relate to Pattie.

Another example could include:

This is a weird situation for Pattie. She is not used to so much attention and listening. She is re-creating with me the feelings that she had with her mother. And she probably feels frightened of me as she felt with her mother. I can move back into my wise Adult self and know she is doing the best she can at this point in time.

Summary

In this chapter, I presented an overview of the activities from the four-step approach that can be used in classrooms, workshop situations, and group and individual supervision. Teachers, supervisors, and facilitators can choose which activities they think will work best for their trainees or group members.

There are a number of benefits to reflecting on countertransference in groups but there are also risks. These risks include group members having countertransference reactions to colleagues' clients and responding in an unprocessed and uncontained way during group discussions. Hence, it is important for classes or groups to discuss how to create a safe environment for reflecting on countertransference prior to engaging in these activities. On the other hand, learning about and reflecting on countertransference in groups can be very rewarding and enhance awareness and understanding of countertransference.

The activities outlined in the chapter (and throughout the book) were adapted for teaching, learning, and reflective practice activities in groups. The activities discussed followed the four-step approach. These included using the PAC model, reflecting on the client's templates for relationships, developing hypotheses about the interpersonal processes, creating empathic self-talk, and moving back into the Adult. These activities were designed to enhance awareness, understanding, and management of countertransference, and to assist therapists to manage the problematic aspects of countertransference, and make use of the benefits of countertransference including understanding our clients more deeply.

Recommended readings

Cartwright, C. & Read, J. (2011). An exploratory investigation of psychologists' responses to a method for considering 'objective' countertransference. *New Zealand Journal of Psychology, 40*, 46–54.

Cartwright, C., Rhodes, P., King, R., & Shires, A. (2014). Experiences of countertransference: Reports of clinical psychology students. *Australian Psychologist, 49*, 232–240.

Cartwright, C., Rhodes, P., King, R., & Shires, A. (2015). A pilot study of a method for teaching clinical psychology trainees to conceptualise and manage countertransference. *Australian Psychologist, 50*, 148–156.

Cartwright, C., Hayes, J. A., Yang, Y., & Shires, A. (2021). 'Thinking it through': Toward a model of reflective practice for trainee psychologists' countertransference reactions. *Australian Psychologist, 56*, 168–180.

References

American Psychological Association (2017). *Ethical principles of psychologists and code of conduct.* Available at: www.apa.org/ethics/code/ (accessed 22 June 2021).

Andersen, S. M. & Berk, M. (1998). Transference in everyday experience: Implications of experimental research for relevant clinical phenomena. *Review of General Psychology, 2,* 81–120.

Aron, L. (1990). One person and two person psychologies and the method of psychoanalysis. *Psychoanalytic Psychology, 7,* 475–485.

Australian Psychological Society (2007). *Code of ethics.* Melbourne, Victoria: APS. Available at: www.psychology.org.au/About-Us/What-we-do/ethics-and-practice-standards/APS-Code-of-Ethics (accessed 22 June 2021).

Bateman, A., Brown, B., & Pedder, J. (2000). *An introduction to psychotherapy: An outline of psychodynamic principles and practices.* London, UK: Routledge.

Beck, A.T. (1976). *Cognitive therapy and the emotional disorders.* New York: International Universities.

Beck, A.T., Freeman, A., & Davis, D. (2004). *Cognitive therapy of personality disorders.* New York, NY: Guilford Press.

Beck, J. (2011). *Cognitive Behavior Therapy: Basics and beyond.* New York, NY: Guilford Press.

Berne, E. (1961). *Transactional analysis in psychotherapy.* New York, NY: Ballantine Books.

Berne, E. (1964). *Games people play: The psychology of human relationships.* New York, NY: Penguin Books.

Betan, E., Heim, A. K., Conklin, C. Z., & Westen, D. (2005). Countertransference phenomena and personality pathology in clinical practice: An empirical investigation. *American Journal of Psychiatry, 162,* 890–898.

Bohart, A. C. & Tallman, K. (2010). Clients: The neglected common factor in psychotherapy. In B. L. Duncan, S. D. Miller, B. E. Wampold, & M. A. Hubble (Eds.), *The heart and soul of change: Delivering what works in therapy* (pp. 83–111). Washington, DC: American Psychological Association.

Bonovitz, C. (2005). Locating culture in the psychic field: Transference and countertransference as cultural products. *Contemporary Psychoanalysis, 41,* 55–75.

Bordin, E. S. (1979). The generalizability of the psychoanalytic concept of the working alliance. *Psychotherapy: Theory, Research & Practice, 16,* 252–260.

Bowlby, J. (1973). *In attachment and loss: Volume II: Separation, anxiety and anger.* London: The Hogarth Press and the Institute of Psycho-analysis.

British Psychological Society (2018). *Code of ethics and conduct.* Available at: www.bps.org.uk/news-and-policy/bps-code-ethics-and-conduct (accessed 22 June 2021).

Broden, M. S. & Agresti, A. A. (1998). Responding to therapists' sexual abuse of adult incest survivors: Ethical and legal considerations. *Psychotherapy: Theory, Research, Practice, Training, 35,* 96–104.

Brown, D. & Pedder, J. (1991). *Introduction to psychotherapy.* London: Tavistock.

Cartwright, C. (2011). Transference, countertransference, and reflective practice in cognitive therapy. *Clinical Psychologist, 15,* 112–120.

Cartwright, C. & Read, J. (2011). An exploratory investigation of psychologists' responses to a method for considering 'objective' countertransference. *New Zealand Journal of Psychology, 40,* 46–54.

Cartwright, C., Rhodes, P., King, R., & Shires, A. (2014). Experiences of countertransference: Reports of clinical psychology students. *Australian Psychologist, 49*, 232–240.

Cartwright, C., Cowie, S., Bavin, L. M., & Bennett-Levy, J. (2019). Therapists' experiences of spontaneous mental imagery in therapy. *Clinical Psychologist, 23*, 225–236.

Cartwright, C., Hayes, J. A., Yang, Y., & Shires, A. (2021). 'Thinking it through': Toward a model of reflective practice for trainee psychologists' countertransference reactions. *Australian Psychologist, 56*, 168–180.

Celenza, A. (2017). Lessons on or about the couch: What sexual boundary transgressions can teach us about everyday practice. *Psychoanalytic Psychology, 34*, 157–162.

Clarkson, P. (1992). *Transactional analysis psychotherapy: An integrated approach.* London: Routledge.

Comas-Diaz, L. (2012). *Multi-cultural care: A clinician's guide to cultural competence.* Washington, DC: American Psychological Association.

Comas-Diaz, L., & Jacobsen, F.M. (1991). Ethnocultural transference and countertransference in the therapeutic dyad. *American Journal of Orthopsychiatry, 61*, 392–402.

Comas-Díaz, L. & Jacobsen, F. M. (1995). The therapist of color and the White patient dyad: Contradictions and recognitions. *Cultural Diversity and Mental Health, 1*, 93–106.

Davis, D. M. & Hayes, J. A. (2011). What are the benefits of mindfulness? A practice review of psychotherapy-related research. *Psychotherapy, 48*, 198–208.

deLara, E.W. (2019). Consequences of childhood bullying on mental health and relationships for young adults. *Journal of Child and Family Studies, 28*, 2379–2389. https://doi.org/10.1007/s10826-018-1197-y

Eichenberg, C., Becker-Fischer, M., & Fischer, G. (2010). Sexual assaults in therapeutic relationships: Prevalence, risk factors and consequences. *Health, 2*, 1018–1026.

Epstein, L. & Feiner, A. (1988). Countertransference: The therapist's contribution to treatment. In B. Wolstein (Ed.), *Essential papers on countertransference* (pp. 282–303). New York, NY: New York University Press.

Erskine, R. (2015). *Relational patterns, therapeutic presence: Concepts and practice of Integrative Psychotherapy.* New York, NY: Routledge.

Fichtner, G. (Ed.) (2003). *The Sigmund Freud–Ludwig Binswanger correspondence 1908–1938.* New York, NY: Other Press.

Flückiger, C., Del Re, A. C., Wampold, B. E., & Horvath, A. O. (2018). The alliance in adult psychotherapy: A meta-analytic synthesis. *Psychotherapy, 55*, 316–340.

Fraley, R. C. & Shaver, P. R. (2008). Attachment theory and its place in contemporary personality research. In O. John & R. W. Robins (Eds.), *Handbook of personality: Theory and research* (3rd edn) (pp. 518–541). New York, NY: Guilford Press.

Freud, S. (1993). Observations on transference-love (1915): Further recommendations on the technique of psycho-analysis III. *Journal of Psychotherapy Practice and Research, 2*, 173–180.

Freud, S. (2003). *An outline of psychoanalysis* (trans. Helena Ragg-Kirkby; intro. Malcolm Bowie). London/New York: Penguin Books.

Freud, S., Strachey, A., & Freud, A. (1973). *The standard edition of the complete psychological works of Sigmund Freud 1856–1939.* London: Hogarth Press.

Gabbard, G. (2001). A contemporary psychoanalytic model of CT. *Journal of Clinical Psychology, 57*, 983–991.

Gabbard, G. (2017). *Long-term psychodynamic psychotherapy: A basic text.* Arlington, VA: American Psychiatric Association.

Gelso, C. (2014). A tripartite model of the therapeutic relationship: Theory, research, and practice. *Psychotherapy Research, 24*, 117–131.

Gelso, C. J. & Carter, J. A. (1985). The relationship in counseling and psychotherapy: Components, consequences, and theoretical antecedents. *The Counseling Psychologist, 13*, 155–243.

Gelso, C. & Hayes, J. (2007). *Countertransference and the therapist's inner experience: Perils and possibilities*. Mahwah, NJ: Lawrence Erlbaum.

Gelso, C. J. & Mohr, J. J. (2001). The working alliance and the transference/counter-transference relationship: Their manifestation with racial/ethnic and sexual orientation minority clients and therapists. *Applied and Preventive Psychology, 10*, 51–68.

Gelso, C. J., Pérez Rojas, A. E., & Marmarosh, C. (2014). Love and sexuality in the therapeutic relationship. *Journal of Clinical Psychology, 70*, 123–134.

Gilbert, P. & Leahy, R. (2007). Introduction and overview: Basic issues in the therapeutic relationship. In P. Gilbert and R. Leahy (Eds.), *The therapeutic relationship in the cognitive behavioral psychotherapies* (pp. 3–23). New York, NY: Routledge.

Gold, J. R. (2013). An integrated approach to the treatment of anxiety. In G. Stricker & J. R. Gold (Eds.), *Comprehensive handbook of psychotherapy integration* (pp. 293–341). Berlin: Springer Science & Business Media.

Gold, J. R. & Wachtel, F. L. (2013). Cyclical psychodynamics. In G. Stricker & J. R. Gold (Eds.), *Comprehensive handbook of psychotherapy integration* (pp. 59–72). Berlin: Springer Science & Business Media.

Goldberg, S. B., Rousmaniere, T., Miller, S. D., Whipple, J., Nielsen, S. L., Hoyt, W. T., & Wampold, B. E. (2016). Do psychotherapists improve with time and experience? A longitudinal analysis of outcomes in a clinical setting. *Journal of Counseling Psychology, 63*, 1–11.

Greenson, R. R. & Wexler, M. (1969). The non-transference relationship in the psychoanalytic situation. *International Journal of Psycho-Analysis, 50*, 27–39.

Halgin, R. & McEntee, D. (2013). Countertransference issues in integrative psychotherapy. In G. Stricker & J. R. Gold (Eds.), *Comprehensive handbook of psychotherapy integration* (pp. 499–512). Berlin: Springer Science & Business Media.

Hayes, J. A. (1995). Countertransference in group psychotherapy: Waking a sleeping dog. *International Journal of Group Psychotherapy, 45*, 521–535.

Hayes, J., Gelso, C., & Hummel, A. (2011). Managing countertransference. *Psychotherapy, 48*, 88–97.

Hayes, J. A., Gelso, C. J., Goldberg, S., & Kivlighan, D. M. (2018). Countertransference management and effective psychotherapy: Meta-analytic findings. *Psychotherapy, 55*(4), 496–512.

Heimann, P. (1950). On counter-transference. *The International Journal of Psychoanalysis, 31*, 81–84.

Hill, C. E., Knox, S., & Pinto-Coelho, K. G. (2018). Therapist self-disclosure and immediacy: A qualitative meta-analysis. *Psychotherapy, 55*, 445.

Hofsess, C. D. & Tracey, T. J. (2010). Countertransference as a prototype: The development of a measure. *Journal of Counseling Psychology, 57*, 52–67.

Horvath, A. O., Re, A. C. D., Flückiger, C., & Symonds, D. (2011). Alliance in individual psychotherapy. In J. C. Norcross (Ed.), *Psychotherapy relationships that work: Evidence-based responsiveness* (pp. 25–69). Oxford University Press.

Kabat-Zinn, J. (2003). Mindfulness-based interventions in context: Past, present, and future. *Clinical Psychology: Science and Practice, 10*(2), 144–156.

Kabat-Zinn, J. (2021). The invitation within the cultivation of mindfulness. *Mindfulness, 12*, 1034–1037.

Kernberg, O. F. (2015). Neurobiological correlate of object relations theory: The relationship between neurobiological and psychodynamic development. *International Forum of Psychoanalysis, 24*, 38–46.

Kiesler, D. J. (1983). The 1982 interpersonal circle: A taxonomy for complementarity in human transactions. *Psychological Review, 90*, 185.

Kiesler, D. (2001). Therapist countertransference: In search of common themes and empirical referents. *Psychotherapy in Practice, 57*, 1053–1063.

Klein, M. (1946). Notes on some schizoid mechanisms. *The International Journal of Psycho-Analysis, 27,* 99–110.

Knifton, L. (2012). Understanding and addressing the stigma of mental illness with ethnic minority communities. *Health Sociology Review, 21,* 287–298.

Koç, V. & Kafa, G. (2019). Cross-cultural research on psychotherapy: The need for a change. *Journal of Cross-Cultural Psychology, 50,* 100–115.

Koocher, G. & Keith-Spiegel, P. (2016). Attraction, romance, and sexual intimacies with clients and subordinates. In G. Koocher & P. Keith-Spiegel, *Ethics in psychology and the mental health professions: Standards and cases* (pp. 275–312). Oxford: Oxford University Press.

Latts, M. & Gelso, C. (1995). Countertransference behaviour and management of countertransference with survivors of sexual assault. *Psychotherapy, 32,* 405–415.

Leahy, R. (2007). Schematic match in the therapeutic relationship: A social cognitive model. In P. Gilbert and R. Leahy (Eds.), *The therapeutic relationship in the cognitive behavioral psychotherapies* (pp. 229–254). New York, NY: Routledge.

Lotterman, J. H. (2014). Erotic feelings toward the therapist: A relational perspective. *Journal of Clinical Psychology, 70*(2), 135–146.

Martin, D., Garske, J., & Davis, K. (2000). Relation of the therapeutic alliance with outcome and other variables: A meta-analytic review. *Journal of Consulting and Clinical Psychology, 68,* 438–450.

McGuire, W. (1974). *The Freud/Jung letters: The correspondence between Sigmund Freud and C. G. Jung.* Princeton, NJ: Princeton University Press.

Millon, G. & Halewood, A. (2015). Mindfulness meditation and countertransference in the therapeutic relationship: A small scale exploration of therapists' experiences using grounded theory methods. *Counselling and Psychotherapy Research, 15*(3), 188–196.

Miranda, R. & Andersen, S. (2007). The therapeutic relationship: Implications for cognition and transference. In P. Gilbert & R. Leahy (Eds.), *The therapeutic relationship in the cognitive behavioral psychotherapies* (pp. 63–69). New York, NY: Routledge.

Mitchell, S. (1988). *Relational concepts in psychoanalysis: An integration.* Cambridge, MA: Harvard University Press.

New Zealand Psychological Society (2012). *Code of ethics for psychologists working in Aotearoa/New Zealand.* Available at: www.psychology.org.nz/members/professional-resources/code-ethics (accessed 22 June 2021).

Newman, C. (2013). *Core competencies in Cognitive-Behavioral Therapy.* New York, NY: Routledge.

Norcross, J. C., Karpiak, C. P., & Lister, K. M. (2005). What's an integrationist? A study of self identified integrative and (occasionally) eclectic psychologists. *Journal of Clinical Psychology, 61,* 1587–1594.

Okamoto, A. & Kazantzis, N. (2021). Alliance ruptures in cognitive behavioral therapy: A cognitive conceptualization. *Journal of Clinical Psychology, 77*(2), 384–397.

Pinto-Coelho, K. G., Hill, C. E., Kearney, M. S., Sarno, E. L., Sauber, E. S., Baker, S. M., ... & Thompson, B. J. (2018). When in doubt, sit quietly: A qualitative investigation of experienced therapists' perceptions of self-disclosure. *Journal of Counseling Psychology, 65,* 440–452.

Racker, H. (1957). The meanings and uses of countertransference. *The Psychoanalytic Quarterly, 26,* 303–357.

Robbins, S. B. & Jolkovski, M. P. (1987). Managing countertransference feelings: An interactional model using awareness of feeling and theoretical framework. *Journal of Counseling Psychology, 32,* 276–282.

Ryle, A. (1998). Transferences and countertransferences: The cognitive analytic therapy perspective. *British Journal of Psychotherapy, 14,* 303–309.

Safran, J. D. (2002). Brief relational psychoanalytic treatment. *Psychoanalytic Dialogues*, *12*, 171–195.

Safran, J. D. & Kraus, J. (2014). Alliance ruptures, impasses, and enactments: A relational perspective. *Psychotherapy*, *51*, 381–387.

Safran, J. & Muran, J. C. (2000). *Negotiating the therapeutic alliance*. New York, NY: Guilford Press.

Safran, J. D., Muran, J. C., & Eubanks-Carter, C. (2011). Repairing alliance ruptures. *Psychotherapy*, *48*, 80–87.

Sandler, J. (1976). Countertransference and role-responsiveness. *International Review of Psycho-analysis*, *3*, 43–47.

Schön, D. (1987). *Educating the reflective practitioner*. San Francisco, CA: Jossey-Bass.

Shafranske, E. & Falender, C. (2008). Supervision addressing personal factors and countertransference. In C. Falender & E. Shafranske (Eds.), *Casebook for clinical supervision: A competency-based approach* (pp. 97–120). New York, NY: American Psychological Association.

Shapiro, S.L., Carlson, L.E., Astin, J.A., & Freedman, B. (2006). Mechanisms of mindfulness. *Journal of Clinical Psychology*, *62*(3), 373–386.

Sonne, J. L. & Jochai, D. (2014). The 'vicissitudes of love' between therapist and patient: A review of the research on romantic and sexual feelings, thoughts, and behaviors in psychotherapy. *Journal of Clinical Psychology*, *70*, 182–195.

Stadter, M. (2016). Time, focus, relationship, and trauma: A contemporary object relations approach to brief therapy. *Psychiatry*, *79*, 433–440.

Stampey, C. D. (2008). Social workers' culture-based countertransferences. *Journal of Ethnic & Cultural Diversity in Social Work*, *17*, 37–59.

Stricker, R. & Gold, J. R. (2013). Assimilative psychodynamic psychotherapy. In J. C. Norcross & M. R. Goldfried (Eds.), *Handbook of psychotherapy integration* (pp. 221–240). Oxford: Oxford University Press.

Tummala-Narra, P., Claudius, M., Letendre, P. J., Sarbu, E., Teran, V., & Villalba, W. (2018). Psychoanalytic psychologists' conceptualizations of cultural competence in psychotherapy. *Psychoanalytic Psychology*, *35*, 46–59.

UK Council for Psychotherapy (2019). *UKCP code of ethics and professional practice*. Available at: www.google.com/search?client=firefox-b-d&q=UK+Council+of+psychotherapy+code+of+conduct (accessed 22 June 2021).

Williams, J. M. G., Teasdale, J. D., Segal. Z. V., & Kabat-Zinn, J. (2007). *The mindful way through depression: Freeing yourself from chronic unhappiness*. New York, NY: Guilford Press.

Winnicott, D. (1949). Hate in the counter-transference. *The International Journal of Psychoanalysis*, *30*, 69–74.

Young, J. E., Klosko, J. S., & Weishaar, M. E. (2003). *Schema therapy*. New York, NY: Guilford Press.

Index